Critical Acclaim

"Stedmond Pardy is an innovator. He writes from a vast knowledge of what has come before him, reasserting literature in his image by challenging the worn-out norms of page poetry and spoken word.

Beached Whales isn't just something new; this is an artist pushing poetics into the future"

-Simon Occulis, the artist formally known as
Brandon Pitts, author of the Gospel of Now and
Tender in the Age of Fury

"In Beached Whales, Stedmond Pardy's second collection of poetry, he continues to startle and engage with his passionate litany of surreal images, observations, and recollections - creating a beautiful and relentless collage of politicized pleas, strained social and sensual intimacies recalled, and aspirations steeped in a kind of glamorous regret and happenstance-cum-hopefulness regarding an undeterminable future. These masterful long-poems culminate and soar into a final soft cry that tentatively and titillatingly suggests that the best, or at the very least, the most *interesting* parts, are yet to come. Evocatively infused with what his Basquiat poem describes as - "Half Erased, cut up words, Pictures, Dropped names, symbols ⬍ ⬍ / Diagrams, References & Facts / scrawled, scRATchEd & LAY-eReD unto tagGed walls", Pardy's new work generously and unabashedly conveys a kind of streetwise religious fervour, Ultimately, the poet becomes his own "loose volcanic nun, vigorously / Rubb[ing] Our Sharp skulls like a / Feathered heart, burnished, by a Drooping, star…"

- David Bateman, Painter, & author of
"Dr.Sad" & "Tis Pity".

From Atlantis to Portugal & Brazil—en route to the future—Stedmond Pardy strikes again with poems of benthic proportions and resonances, converging myth with visions of a world un-coerced by capital, urging wakefulness to the challenges of our time. Pardy's poems embolden "by speaking nakedly to your soul."

~ Adebe DeRango-Adem, author of
Vox Humana (Book*hug Press, 2022)

BEACHED WHALES

BEACHED WHALES

by

Stedmond Pardy

Library and Archives Canada Cataloguing in Publication

Title: Beached whales / by Stedmond Pardy.

Names: Pardy, Stedmond, 1983- author.

Description: Poems.

Identifiers: Canadiana (print) 20230510574
              Canadiana (ebook) 20230510582

ISBN 9781771617123 (softcover) ISBN 9781771617130 (PDF)
ISBN 9781771617147 (EPUB) ISBN 9781771617154 (Kindle)

Classification: LCC PS8631.A7415 B43 2023 | DDC C811/.6—dc23

Published by Mosaic Press, Oakville, Ontario, Canada, 2024.

MOSAIC PRESS, Publishers
www.Mosaic-Press.com
Copyright © Stedmond Pardy 2024

Printed and bound in Canada.

MOSAIC PRESS
1252 Speers Road, Units 1 & 2, Oakville, Ontario, L6L 5N9
(905) 825-2130 • info@mosaic-press.com • www.mosaic-press.com

Dedication

This Book is Dedicated to You,
whoever YOU are reading it ..NOW.

Contents

"It HURTS but THAT'S ...Baseball"

My Mom, was knocked
                    Up
with me when she was
                    15 &,
Had me, when she was
                    ...16,
& the 1st pink snow fall of the
Season always brings tears
to Her 3rd
Eye,
As She saunters (Iconically)
within ... It.

I adore the way you, Say:
"Papillon". While we lay pieta'd,
In the consoling tentacles of a
secret, Fortified luxurious underground
Doomsday bunker, hunkering under the
Fertile Lombard plains
of your warm,
Queen sized bed, on cold
Winter morns in the shadowy!
Doom laden, hyper kinetic,
Blue lotus Blossom
shaped, price gouge-ing
Cities tranquil,
Untilled, coagulated, plasma coated fields
of the Impaled,
Where almost every single

1

Thing,
That was once soooooo much,
Fun, has been regulated
Sooo asphyxiating
-ly, that it has now been Re
-developed, into something quite,
LAME.
As the white! Oracular crows
of -Something- no
medium can seemingly ever
Manage to Adequately "Define",
Flew-ABOVE...
& 124 suspected Arms dealers,
Sex Traffickers, Pedophiles, &
Crack, meth, & Fentanyl Distributing
Gang members from North York
(& else where in the GTA) were found fetus'd
In the trunks of their cars, stabbed,
Beaten --horrifically, & shot,
14 times each (like Antonio Caponigro),
with money stuffed into their
mouths &, Anus's,
by karma, Hermes,
John Rambo, Contemporary
Travis Bickle's, &Neglectful,
     Unaffectionate,
Neglectful, regret ridden ...
Parents...

Through Stormy, Post bio digital
Seas,
where no desperate sail before
was ever hoisted, under 6 Ribbed
Vaulted arches of a
Flattened,
Octagonal dome of Liquid, wood,
Painted by an anomalous song
nobody has had the rare, exquisite!

Monumental Privilege of hearing
Get played! Orches
-trated in that unwendable, Idiosyncratic
Way NOBODY,
other than you, Can play…it, is
The only place that is habitable
now, & Hasn't been, Dep
-leted for Us, Who'd rather become
Calcinated ashes, then get Reduced, to
Stale… Dust…

To Wittle away "the Inessentials" &
A-Symptomatic spread,
--T - T- To unshackle our quadruple
Headed Eagles, from an
Unclamberable, maenad Haunted
Mountain of melted-Iron,
Lettuce greened by a mammatus
cloud capped!
Blue moonscape of a regenerative
silent,
Everlasting SPRING roused! Out
of the Big, mouth, watering reveries
It was once, encapsulated.
      In, Snugly!
& release our Famished!! Bengal
Tigers out of the Stultifying, Abu
Gharib-esque Cage of a
Tiny… Bird… Frightened into Blind
Obedience,
Numbness, & A Remarkable, Convenient
Loss …of, Memory…

My Mother, was knocked up with
ME<
      When she was…15, & had
"Me",
      When she was "16",

& when i dropped out of, school! There was
Only 1 solar, system! & Pluto,
was STILL, Considered,
A "Planet".

I adore the Way you,
    Say,

"PAPILLON"…During
Whatever comes
…After!
      The Kali
             Yuga/ "The
Iron AGE, of
          Hesiod"…

Beached Whales 2

I am Not! Supposed to be Stuck
"Here".

I should be somewhere in Portugal
As I write this, dear reader,
Letting my Famished
Inner tiger out of the
Tiny,
Abu gharib-ic cage of a Bird,
Not growing roots & rust in isolation,
somewhere in Toronto- "Standing
Together! By Staying
Ap-ar-t"! My
Icarus-ian Wings, of
Steel, Clipped, by Covid-19, unable to
perform or WORK, unable
to go to the *movies*, unable
to listen to live music, unable
to venture to a coffee shop, Library,
Church, Restaurant, gym or, Bar.

Goose stepping into the Gulbenkien, NMAA, Art Deco &
Aljube museums, Terraced
Vineyards, & Bustling, scent filled Bakeries
is what "I" should, be doing,
"I" should,

be at the statue of Pessoa, outside
The Cafe A Brasileria, right now,
The tomb of Vasco Degamos. The

Chapel of St.john The
Baptist
or some structure, created by
Nicolau Nasoni is
Where "i" now, should Be!!

Balls deep in the birthplace
of FADO in an intimate,
Charming, Candlelit cafe listening
to … FADO, on my 3rd bottle
of Vinho Verde, understanding the true
meaning of the word "Saudade", crossing,
Strolling the Dom Luís I Bridge & the 15 mile
Long, 25th of April Bridge or in a Ginjinha Bar!
Exploring Villas, Cathedrals, Ruined Medieval
Castles, & Forts
… "Unparalled in Antiquity" On
Black & white cobble stone side`
walks eating a
BIFANA! a Bolas de berlim, Francesinha,
Pastel De nata, & Bacalhau,
Having my OWN visions
of Fatima, is what i should
at this moment be, Doing,
Not uninspired, at 3 with myself,
& the world, wondering who would
win if William Burroughs battled
Valerie Solanas? the Cassius Green's of the globe
square-ing off against the Adrian Veidt's?
Wondering if I made an ecstatic Fool of
myself at a gathering
of friends, that i wasn't even really
Invited to… i shouldn't be stranded, Here!
In Toronto, or anywhere near
The province of Ontario, Worrying
That i may never be able to,
Escape
… it?

I was supposed to be witnessing the sunset on
a Sandy beach, in Nazare. On
a Trolley enroute, to Score some
"K",
Or in the Oldest Beer hall in Lisbon. In
A port wine cellar shining!! Across
the Duoro river,
Browsing the Book shelves
at "Lello & Irmao" & Livraria Bertrand,
Purchasing fresh sun dried fish from
the wives of, Fishermen,
Wishing i was aboard a ship in
the poetic epic "The Lusaids", witnessing
(chastely) women in traditional
garments, exiting iconic colored
tile Buildings digging the Street
 art, Writing joyful, detail laden, letters
to cherished names to me, forever!
Dear,
from the Rooftop of my Air B'N'B
…Halfway to Sintra (wreathed in mist), Coimbra
or Belem, is what i
Dreamed i'd be doing (with you)
under new skies, for
more than a year but now,
can't!

Today, July 20th, 2020, I would have
been in Portugal, Blessed by our lady
of Good Health, packing my bags for my
overdue pilgrimage, to the graves of 2 of my
Heroes, buried in Rome before My
Convergence, at the Cinema al Belvedere,
with my own, ever drifting, Mrs.
Stone, dear reader.

I'm Not supposed to be stranded,

"Here".

By an Emerald fire

1.

Awa-Away from the flaky, photoshopped
Denizens of the DatingApps,
Awa- Away, from the desecrating
        cat's Paw of the vampiric powers
        that be, & the smug, surveillance capitalists
        Hollow, Lurid,
        Beckoning, devitalizing spectacle, away, from
        the suffocating grasp of the narcissistic, philanthropic
        Billionaire ventriloquists' staged
        managed perceptions evangelists,
        Social validation feed back
        ...Loops,
        & the rigged game being
        UPPED.

Awa-Away from Our solidified thick, Long white,
        shadows &
        THEIR Bogey man's
        Red herrings agent, provocateurs,
        Crying...Wolf....

From the sacred medicine dens of Andromeda,
    & Czechoslovakia,
from Forced production, to gross, wasteful over
    Consumption, from Pay check to Pay
    Check,

from Paste to, powder to, Rock, &
& Chakra, to
  Chakra, tooth, to
Nail, Lip to Ear,
Diaper to diaper, Pernambuco to Porto, Lisbon
 & Shade to SHADE,
To the top hatted Capitalist regions
  Of Afghan, & Pakistan, & the Moon,
To the white waters of…Atlantis,
Through Soil, moisture, Root damage,
  & Strong winds,
Through the gruelling process of, -Individuation- &
  Beyond,
In the Monet-ic Morning,
Van gogh-ian GANGSTERS!!!
  Of -The Starry Night-,
AWOKE<
  To See
A Universe of Ghost
Shadows,
  In a Cloud of smoke, being,
Blown by the
Beautiful!
  Death killing, Beauties,
Chanting
  The Lost poems,
Of every known,
  & Unknown poet,
  To
The 27th centuries cave MEN,
& their Ravishing rave Women,
  who are
Communicating in
Neanderthal symbols, & Grunts,
 To their Cave, Rave
  Runts!
Playing & Dancing, by an Emerald
  Fire,

Openly grieving the day,
That their Earthly lives, will
Never EXPIRE, Inside,
The marshmallow, Mountain, Iced,
    With Pink
        …SNOW.

2.

Polluters of the Planet,
& Dark, Intro -spective,
Voyeurs of the Soul,
Living in Opulent,
Furnished under
-ground Bunkers,
Like worms, Hitler,
Gophers & Moles, feeling
All GROOO -VVVYYY YYY,
Laughing, Cack -ling,
at our lives Movies,
With their Distracted, info
Barraged Brains,
Coddled like New born
Despots, in the cold,
Blankets of Enlight
-enmen
       t,
Tip toe ballerina-ing through
The neutered villages, of
      Soft!
Half eaten GLASS!
Ballerina toe-ING through the soft,
Neutered
      Tip,
of Glass villages, HALF
    Eaten, soft

Ballerina-ing through the villages,
of Eaten glass neutered,
Through Toe-ing,
      TIP?

Beached Whales 3 (aka"Jack Dempsey Fought to Do more than Just Win")

You:

"COERCE"-
Means to compel by FORCE, Intimidation,
Or Authority,
Especially devoid in regard for personal Desire or,
                                        Volition,
-The application of Strong, ARM, tactics-
"I can be your best, Friend or, your WORST
...Enemy!?"
Its "Rexall" versus "Shoppers Drug mart?" My heart,
"Bell" or "Rogers", "Black Rock Inc" or "The Vanguard
-Group", my sweet,
It's "Don't you ever let me hear that again, or I'll
Lose my temper, Vito"
"You are either with ME!! Or You're Against,
ME?"
"You are either with US!! Or You're
With the... terrorists/ Communists/ Racists or
Baby Eating DEMONS?"
"It's Either an Aristotelian
THIS, or Its a mono
-chromatic THAT"! REPENT,
& worship what I/WE, worship, or PERISH?
"Surrender or... Else"
If you LOVE ...me ...You'll- do
...This?"
"It's Mister Joe, or ....ME, Louis?"

"If You didn't get all the Covid Shots, you can't come
to family Dinner"

Me:

COERCION,
To achieve an Aim by Muscle or threat, Menace, or
Pressure, "COERCE",
To hold in, Restrain! To shut up, To "Manipulate",
Sequester,
To anger, confuse, fetter, repress, Div-ide, noicreoC,
To Neuter, Spay Marginalize, Excoriate,
Bureaucratize! Commodify, Castrate, Enclose! Deplete.
Regiment, Manacle, Muzzle, Shackle, en
-slammer, lap dog, Errand boy/girl,
& Malgovern, chronically!
Coercion!
What's mine is MINE, & what's yours &... theirs,
Is ALSO... Mine!
COERCION,
under the guise of the greater good.

You:

Coercion,
To Starve & PARCH into
"Submission", & compliance,
Coercion,
To Water down, Dilute, & Declaw, De
-BEAK, Coercion! To importune, Minimize, Impede,
To program, Stage manage, & cordone off, ineptly,
& undertake the ruthless ritual strangling of
Every potential, budding leader while they are
Still babes babbling in their CRIBS,
& be
The gluttonous worm, fattening itself
Inside the rotten core,
of every- Blue Apple, To Be

The proverbial rusty nail, in every overly expensive, yet
Cheaply made shoe,
noicreoC?
To drain the resources, & life blood out of all continents,
Coercion,
To suck the heart, mind & numbed, strategically
Distracted soul
out of a once VIBRANT, thriving community,
& try to privatize, water? Electricity, property, Education, Health care,
science,
Sustenance, " The Truth", Rain forests, Consciousness, Solutions, etc.
Coercion
"I was just following orders"
noicreoC?
"I was only doing what I was told to ...Do!
Why should I be held accountable for my
Actions or, lack there of?"

Me:

Coercion,
To Have to age according to a Calendar a calendar Conc
-octed By a POPE, noicreoC?
To subvert, Infiltrate, Distract, Neutralize,- Mis
-direct! Fillet,
Coercion,
To Pin, under a "Contractual" Thumb,
   & put under the yolk, To-
To Have to be well adjusted to a twisted, asphyxiating
Conception of the
World.
& wrench another Organisms Arm into passively, accepting
WHO,
While making them become the unwitting instruments of ...WHAT?
noicreoC!
To thwart personal growth, & lasting, much needed change, Coercion!
To En-Crony, to En-shill,
To try to transform a bountiful paradise into a, brutal sweat shop,

Or a barren "land of excessive, waste"
Coercion,
To rub pink Himalayan salt, & Dried Jalapeño peppers,
into EVERY open...Wound,
& have to respond to a whistle, Phone call, text, bell,& the snap
-ping, of some pricks, dirty Fingers.

You:

Noicreoc?
The Imposition of Crippling economic, Sanctions,
Coercion,
"Who has the Smallest cock?" &
"Who'll Use the Most Lube!?" are the 2
main Questions to ask yourself before you ever –Vote~
noircreoC?
Favoured, over privileged classes/
Specialized groups,
Coercion,
A
Dioramic tavern of an inflamed Camels BLUSHING! DIS
-colored Skull, &
FREED, skim milk colored NEGROES,
Synchronizing 70's Porno, to...MUSIC, Ink black Caucasians
Rowing dragon boats,
Through WOODEN water...A
Congested city blowing it's Snotty,
Nose- Coercion, "By
Lunch time on January
1st!
The Highest paid CEOS in
North America will have scrounged, the Equivalent of
Our yearly Wages".
COERCION!
The huge, wetted Beak, & grease coated palms,
Noicreoc!
Catalogues of Horror(s)! Montages of...
"Atrocities",

"Appetite for Destruction", Recipes,
for ...Disaster. COER
-CION!

Me:

Love Gun to Head, HEAD, Butter knife to throat! THROAT, Polar
Opposite of Liberty! Advertisings Subliminal
Sorcery at Work,
Appalling obstructions of "Justice"-
LADY MACBETH, & the devitalizing narrowers of
The boggling Immensity of
Life,
Hoarking Phlegm upon the ghosts of Harry J
Anslinger & J.p Morgan,
Josef Stalin, William Randolph Hearst,
J.Edgar Hoover, Duncan Campbell Scott, Christopher
Columbus, Bindy Johal,
Anita Bryant, Ariel Sharon, Yasar Arafat! Baruch Goldstein
The Marco's lol Francisco Franco!
John A. Macdonald, Arthur Mitchell Sackler!
Emperor Hirohito! The Dulles' Brothers,
Mao Zedong, Napoleon! Idi Amin, Papa & Baby Doc Duvalier!
The Patriarchs of the 12 riches families in ...The World!
Adolf Hitler, George H.W Bush, Pablo Escobar, Adrian Veidt,
António de Oliveira Salazar & the Flag of, Every country as I, Laugh,
Unceasing conun-drums, Rigid Orthodoxy,
Compulsory PROSTITUTION,
Unreasonable Searches &
... Seizures-
Joe Pesci in "Casino", Wizards of symbols &
"Semantics", Aydin Coban & Matthew Hopkins
Pry
-ing open (with the help of fierce horse
Women of the bright side of the Moon) a Mouth Forever
Closed, "Spiritual
Intrusion!"
Spiritual Black mail!

Chronic revisionism & food insecurity,
"Unspecified abuses of power",
Militarized Police, Snuffed, Missing Journalists, yellow
Journalism!! "BLACK Propaganda",
Arrested Defenders of Indigenous LAND, Quashed Protests, Busted
Unions,
Planned obsolescence, Conflicts of Interest, Parasitic
Perpetuators of a vile, unsustainable ---System!
"Vacuous WOKEness", the Military industrial Complex,
...Signaled virtue?
Taxation WITHOUT *Representation* Big Pharma! Big TECH,
The Fossil Fuel Industry,
& the Serious possibility of Monstrous legal Penalties
If YOU, & a 96 Year old Woman
Swal
-lowing a Black diamond mauling an ENORMOUS Pitbull
BBQ'd in a California Limo
Fire,
Attempt to Do (or say, or Post)…"THIS?"

You:

"COERCE"-
To Lower in Character, Quality,
Or Value,
To have to fit into "their" mold or ELSE get, shunned-
"noicreoC"?
The Rub & tug Masseuses embarrassed,
Long, Suffering, en-lab ratted Father …Famished amidst,
PLENTY, A
Gigantic Non-entity, Composed of nearly 7 Billion People-A
Feral Kitten!!!
Licking it's own thick long white, solidified Shadow, on Our
curved, load bearing Wall,
I Begin to sprint, slither, crawl, Lurch! Skip, WALK!!! In
On The Velvet Underground Recording "Sister Ray", "SISTER
RAY"!
& My Clothes Change... 60

Times!, noicreoC!
"In Order to Date, Me" She said "You'll Have to Drive
A Half Decent Car,
Own or Rent a Spectacular Home, Befriend My Vicious,
Semi Contemptuous Friends & Family "Owling" Your every
Move, Pet my horribly trained, Pets,
& BE FINANCIALLY SECURE at the expense
Of Your Soul & Mind" They
Said,
You are going to have to do THIS,
You are goingta' HAVE to wear one of these to
Do ...that?
"You are going to Need a Credit card to Pay for, THIS, sir".
 "You'll Have to get yerself a Bank account in order
To be able to work.......HERE". Coercion,
Narrowed horizons, Lowered expectations, &
Factory model schooling,
COERCION,
"Our rights are never more fragile
then in times,
of National Emergency", "These are the dispiriting Times
that try OUR Souls". noicreoC!
there is no instance in history when Censorship
& secrecy have advanced either Democracy,
or... Public health,
COERCION

Me:

i don't know what else to say! They got us thrusting knives
at each others throats & backs over cookie
crumbs, while
they are pulling out the silverware at LAVISH, all you can eat -buffets!
...Liberated modern, Homo
-phobic House wives are still calling Gay men, being told
They have to go to College, or University & get in a,
Fuck load of Debt, in order to be able
To Get a Good, Job,

"Pillow Biters" & ... "Shit Dicks!??!"
Passable Transgender Women carrying Water
Guns full of Whiskey are Bullying
MEAN Lesbi-ans, Astride a, Soiled Dove! Our
Unconditional Love, is Commercials! Taxes! Killer
Snowmen? "Change"! MYSELF! Politics, Stupidity,
Hypocrisy! CHICANERY< construction, greed,
Corporate malfeasance, Other people's Smart,
Phones?
I Can't Escape, it! COERCION,
"Silent weapons for Quiet Wars"? a "PSYOP" is
a _Censored-
   Was the unabomber right about the future of Tech?
"False flag" events, Are "------Fear
Mongering is "The Use of FEAR, ignorance, & superstition to influence
The opinions & Actions of others, towards
Some Specific- End",
MAMMON is Bible riches, Avarice, &
Worldly Gain,
Personified as a False God in the "New Testament", FREEDOM,
Is "The Power or Right to act, Speak, or think as one wants without
Hindrance or Restraint,
Political, Religious, or National Independence,
The ABSENCE of Necessity, Coercion, or Constraint in Choice,
Or Action". "We Live in a Time when Inferior Men
& Women are in Power every
where!"
"A Hobson's choice is an apparently free Choice,
That is no Choice at
All".
"Coprophagia" is a word that means the Consumption
Of Feces!& Fecalphiliacs, are people who love to Shove said
Substance into their faceless Mouths,
& For about..99% of "US", to Scrrrrrrrrappppeeee, By
Nowadays,
We Will have to consume a lot of, IT! As You,
Know, so

Let's Dig, IN...Knives, Forks, Spoons! Chopsticks!
.....Hands......

You:

Humankind has "Foolishly allowed their public servants to
Become their Masters"! COERCION,
The FIX is ..IN,
"This May be The Hour when the sacred is Leaving the
Earth", Will we let, it?
What is Supposed to Have been a transcendent,
Awe inspiring Experience,
Has long become a Sick,   Joke,
noicreoC!

To Restrain, or dominate, DOMINATE! By Force, Sinister
Intelligence! & Bodily threat, OR! The
Strategic withholding, of
CERTAIN, Essential, pleasures!! Coercion, To spade, neuter, Castrate,
Grope, GOOSE<
To En-mercenary, to en SICKen, to Marginalize,
To .... Fustigate! Railroad, EnGNARL. NOICREOC .
If we reap what we SOW, & Karma truly,
Exists! what, as a species, do we got hurtling
toward us like a few Stray, Hollow point
Bullets, dipped in POISON... Coercion.

Me:

To Swing a Water worn Minoan axe, ShAtTeRiNg into Damp
Leaves in, Mansions of
Eczeyma Infected, Synthetic...
Skin,
To HAVE to act against one's own Wishes in
"Their" Edenic! Carnivalesque, dystopia, & a hall of, dusty Mirrors,
in a muddy labyrinth Where

Our crushed Dreams, come, TRUE
...noicreoC ?

You:

To Subvert, Infiltrate, Distract, Neutrailize, Mis
-direct- Devitalize, Commodify, collar, DEPLETE, Fillet, Repress,
noicreoC!?

To Compel to an Act, or Hobson's
Choice,

You & Me/ "Us" (at the same time):

To Despotize! DRAGOON? Browbeat! Extort? Mani
-pulate, Indenture, Stigmatize,
EXPLOIT, Homogenize, Mandate?Goad! Standardize!
Bridle...De-platform...TeRrOrIzE...Coa
X"

Burnt Plastic

A
Snowstorm opened wide it's white
Wings over the shadowy, doom laden,
Hyperkinetic, Blue lotus blossom
Shaped city
of liquid, speckled! Philosophic
Stone,
As he fell into a coma, & a flightless bird,
Was body checked by the other side
Of the North,
          Wind…

          6
Million leap year babies celebrated
Their long awaited Birthdays,
& a starving pack of coyote wolf hybrids,
POUNCED, upon our
Jubilant, un
          -suspecting Hikers…

Archaic Places (again) Perished into
"Modernity",
When He slipped into a coma, & our
Usain Bolt, Donovan Bailey Legged
Summers, Wilted,
Into the   Past.   "Nothing-

"Nothing could have prepared the kids
& Parents assembled in the Auditorium for

22

What they were about to
Experience that Night". When He made
The courageous, Death
Defying Leap, into the "Virginal Region", for which,
There exists, No Map.

      I Colla
         p-
I collapsed like an exhausted, paralytic
Sprinter in the dark, Enchanted, chain sawed,
Crystal beast haunted forests of my mind,
I sat, perched, upon the stumps of
Walking, Leafless! Snow covered
Trees, consigned, to the wood
Chipper- I
Made voodoo dolls of all my friendly
Enemies real, & Imagined-
& placed an inexorcisable curse upon,
Everyone, with whom I ever went to
School, with, &, sealed it, in
      Blue, blood...

Gluttonous! Unredeemable, unmitigated Scumbags
Received the Royal treatment, when he fell, into
A Coma, & generous, gorgeous
Souled individuals got treated worse than
Giant Octopuses, Invading, San
Francisco,
& the aborted Babies!!! Who are now in Catholic
Heaven... All grown,
       Up.

      A
Storm of snow, opened wide it's white,
Wings, over the shadowy, doom laden,
Hyperkinetic, blue lotus blossom
Shaped city,

& A flightless bird, got body checked, by
The other side of the North
-wind.(East of the
Sun)
As he slipped into a, Coma. "Nothing-

"Nothing could have prepared the kids
& Parents assembled in the auditorium for
what they were about to experience
that night," When He
Made the courageous, Death defying Leap,
Into the "Virginal Region", for which
There exists, no map...

6

Million leap year babies Recuperated from
Celebrating, their long awaited,

Birthdays,
& the starving pack of Coyote wolf, Hybrids,
DIGESTED, the remains,
Of our Jubilant, Unsuspecting –Hikers,

As his last remaining, relatives told the Doctor,
        To Pull- the plug.

Dahteste (a Poem written in Montreal 2)

When I went to School there was only -One-
Solar-system, & Pluto, was
-STILL- a Planet,
The Sun, slouched at a -Rakish Angle- in the Ind
-ifferent sky, back then, it shone brightly, brightly
through our
SHaTtErEd window,
& a loose volcanic nun, vigorously
                Rubbed
Our Sharp skulls like a
Feathered heart, burnished, by a
Drooping, star,
In Quaint Villages, shaded by immense,
        Walking, leafless,
Snow covered trees.
& a laboratory in Switzerland, created the
ghost of James Joyce, where the
-Gay winds stayed to woo the young
        Lovers as they Passed-
Even, then, & even then, I,
        KNEW< that
 -The old Fruit must, rot!
For the New Seed(s) to take, Root -Even, Then! & even
Then I, KNEW,
That everything! That we have
Been going through! …Recent
-ly,
is Just, -the unabated Storm before the
        -Calm-

Even then, & even back then i
Worried, that -They- might try to do to ME,
& You?
What they did to most of our lost,   Heroes or,
Made most of THEM, Do … To, THEM …Selves…
During what comes
                        after! the Iron age/ Kali
                            …Yuga, when
Humankinds' collective, desiccated, De
        -beaked
Chickens, come -Home,
                                to
        ROOST…

Grusinskaya

"The Women of Algiers in Their Apartment"
"The Women of Algiers in Their Apartment"
"The Women of Algiers in Their Apartment"
"The Women of Algiers in Their Apartment"
"THE WOMEN OF ALGIERS IN THEIR
Apartment!!"
At the Beginning of this Poem I have
Just silkscreened /reproduced the title of my
Favourite Painting(next to Rubens "3 graces" & Basquiat's
          "Baptism" or "Pegasus")
5 times.

On June 10ᵗʰ, On June 10ᵗʰ,
          1987,
The Day before My sister Amanda was
Born, the
Actress Elizabeth Hartman committed
          Suicide
By sky diving out of her 5th story Window-
          On July 22ⁿᵈ, On
July 22ⁿᵈ!! 1934, "I" was
Gunned down in front of "The
Biograph theatre" as I fantasized
About ˝Ó◈ ÚÎ◊₁$^{}?"
& The portrait of The St. Patricks day of The
World of the- Spirit, & Baron Samedi
Coddling a Unicorn!   "I
HAVE JUST COME FROM THE ST.JAMES
          THEATRE"!

Declared Orson Welles,
"Where I have been Murdering Desdemona,
      OR, Shakespeare,
Depending on which Newspaper you read"
            MY
Kindergarten self catches a sneak peek of
            ME
Being strangled by a Python
In my sleep, now!
      & starts to, cry-
Snow plows race through
The frigid avenues of late summer with the
Intellect of
Douche bags &,
Lewd Vagrants Rioting because
Their.... Favourite...sports...teams lost
The championship
      "Game"!

... Ballet!? Modernly
Danced Ballet is assisting some
Autistic girl reconnect to
         The Multidimensional World, around
--Her,
& a Technologically over stimulated Woman,
Wearing the "Cloak of, Shame", In
      "The Act of Faith"!
Is tying up Rush hour traffic, in a
      Pretty little,
         Bow...
 "Hesiod! & The Muses!" "Hesiod
& The, Muses",
Hesiod & The Royal Womb watch? The Royal!!
Womb...   WATCH!!!

... Long before I ever emerged from
Out of the Crotch, of My Orange
            Haired Swedish Women

Who's Talismanic Presence holds the
Destructive forces of a "Stuffed bald
Eagle
Carrying a Rope attached to a, Pillow",
At!! Bay, Long
     Before I ever EXPLOD-ed from
Out of the Mangled!
Lab grown TW@T of my Orange haired, Swedish
Women Speaking English with a Prussian
          Accent
Sprawling on the freshly mown Silver grass, neigh
  -bouring
a Purple Pond of Uncouth
    TWIST!! Gl- Glistening with
…Dew,
I was well aware of a stylish Yakuza with
Tuberculosis who wishes there were
More people in this world, Like
     ….you,
I was well aware of the STARK fact that the
Symbol of the performance of the act
    Of Living is,
Dance! & that the ancient symbol of Human
Aspiration toward the universal, good, is
The BURNT BRIDGES pushed envelopes being
    LICKED,
By Amber Waves' EYES!

Greta Ga-
Greata Garbo, was the Immigrant fury of my
Coagulated lusts brutal feather, uprooted
Christmas trees left up all year,
     Round!
& the violet blood covered Lances of Our Barren
    Moonscape,
Of Disconsolate, eyes!
Greta Lovisa Gustaffson was a great distillation

Of, clotted- joy!
Greta Garbo, who left "Nothing" to be desired,
Had Magnificent "eyes"!
& was exactly what a star SHOULD
        Be!
Robert Sherwood, once wrote "She is the Dream
Princess of Eternity, The Knockout!
Of the Ages"
John Gilbert said that she was
     "Marvellous!!
The Most Alluring Creature you
   Have ever seen" Transmuting
Genetically Modified emotion into Cas
     -cading
SOUND.

Polytonal Egyptians Communicating via
Or
Around Quadraplegiac Dancers running! HOPPING,
   Skipping, Jumping!
Conceptually LUNGE-ing into fresh fields of
   Characterization mope-ing around the
Gorilla haunted streets with the Indecent ease
Of our Diminutive GIANT< Dom
-esticating Women & - Bears &…Flies!
"Immortalized" in Cement-
     hErOiC ViLLaiNs…
Stroking the embroidered, body!! Of a
   BrO-k-E-n Cello,

…Dehydrated, FOXES, of the
   Smog
Choked… Plains.

The Bandits

Sharon & Carl were 2
Beautiful, Robin hood like
Thieves from the East Coast,
Who suffered from Addiction,
& Could procure you anything
You needed, to Support....
Their Habits ...

Work boots, Dress pants, jeans,
Shoes, Razors, Perfumes & Colognes,
Big bottles of Booze, Whole
Seasons of shows Video games,
Movies, What do you want?
Silk, or satin sheets? Do you need Books
from Chapters Indigo? Jackets
Of sports teams, & Leather!?
Power tools? what? A case of beer?
Board games? Cake Mixers?
Milk shake maker? toys?
All Antiquities sacred monuments,
Thick, Unfathomable Black
Chaos' Diadem? &
Great cuts of Meat !?!
Art supplies?
You name... it, they could get ... it
For...... you, & usually
Did, Making
Happy the Birthdays,
Christmases, Easters, Anniversaries,

Valentines days Hannukkahs &,
Kwanzaas, of the less Fortunate,
& Needy, with their apartment, Motel Rooms
& Car full, of, pilfered,
        Merch…

     … Inimitable! Robin hood like Characters,
       Such, as you & I & others will never
       Stagger across again, who's Benevolent
       Exploits cannot, anymore,
       Be Equaled. Beautiful, Unforgettable,
       Robin hood like Thieves from
       The East Coast, Who's passing
       Is the ending, of a
Gleaming era. It was them & one
Other, who got me the transformative
       Texts I needed to turn me into a left
       Handed poet, Instead of a grow op
Employee, & street pharmacist. Just
       As My Fortunes were about to, change…
       For the worst. I even mentioned them
The first time I read my poetry,
& was Interviewed by Nik Beat On HOWL
       89.5fm,
       When I moved downtown, losing touch
       Though, I still heard say! Tell of
       Their Legend fading due to
       Anti theft measures, Occasional
  Prison, ILLNESS…

       …. After a Courageous, heroic Battle
with Cancer, Sharon passed into
Spirit, On the 1st of May, & Carl,
       Joined her, 5 days later, of
A suspected overdose, just like
He once claimed he'd

Do, If she were to Succumb….
        He kept his word, I guess, Symbiotic,
Was their strange, union… & due
To the Covid-19, Wu Han virus,
I, You, & Other beneficiaries of theirs,
        Over the Decade(s), Aren't able to
Properly pay our respects, & say
A final "goodbye", or a heartfelt

      "Thanks".

So here in Quarantine, During
This Global Pandemic
     … On a grey
Rainy day before Mothers day
Weekend, I'm pouring myself the
Last of My "Dillons" Brand
     "Absinthe",
For Brunch. To Salute the
Generous lives of two, Unfor
-gettable, Beautiful! Robin
Hood like, Thieves, along
     With our Other, Lost Sain--

Mushy, distant, Athenian, Peach Colored Marble

"The Lord of the Skies"
was also Known, as the
King of the White Gold, &
"Those Who want to Build
Themselves some Muscles
Don't Lift-feathers"

Rhythmic Talons are trimming
Melancholy, Sepulchres!
& Consoled
Bloodless wings, are frightening
Mushy, Distant! Athenian,
Peach Colored
- Marble...

Punch Drunk from squandering Our
Most valuable Commodities (Focus
& TIME) gawking at a
Dazzling view, of an Internal -Caribbean,
& ALL sides, of a Dracula-ian Screen
with men & Women &
OTHERS,
Grooming themselves like alley
Cats in the monastic cave temples
CARVED, into the indian Cliff sides
& Feeding themselves
as if they are all

Flightless birds
Behind the HEAVY, iron curtain
of MEAT, & Green
Door
when New York, Las Vegas, Macau,
& Dubai- SLEEP...

A Mandarin Duck is sniffing,
Powderized water off of the
Wet back! of
a BLOATED! Self replicating
Monster with a Chlorophyll based
Nervous system, comprised of 8
Billion People (at each others slit
Throats) over paltry crumbs & Hollow
ideologies, licking the moist,
Birth canal of the mortal coil
of a Quivering,
Criminally underrated, Contronymic,
Grandmother fresh out of
The Polished oak, & Poached ivory
Panelled Cocoon,
Becoming the infallible empress, the un
Sniperable, Queen! of
ALL,
I survey, using Capoeiristas as Hit
Men, & Bodyguards, outside a
Reddened Room full, of
Silhouetted,
Partially digested people riding
...Excer...cise...Bikes...
After consuming far TOO much
ic-ich-Ichor aboard
a Metallic, borrowed skin covered,
sea
Horse shaped, ship, gifted with
FLIGHT...

Every Night & day! The Much needed rainfall
Tetra Morphs our pink packing
Snow into the
Poignant winter, frost!
Slaughtering our EVER...greens...beyond all
Computation, Alphabets! speculation &
MATH.

Resurrected mummies & a claustrophobic
Man suffering the delirium tremens at rush
hour aboard a packed bus,
Sought vengeance upon the callous
Archeologists, who invaded their
Lovers looted--Tomb.

Menacing HUGE, Diamond hearted,
giggly,

Outlaw bikers escorted a
Bullied, developmentally challenged
Girl to school, & One of my nieces
Put polysporin &, Liquid Soap, upon
the Tooth Brushes of Her sister &,
MINE.

Those who want to Build themselves some
Muscles, don't
Lift FEATHERS &, The Lord of the
Skies,
was the King, of the WHITE
gold.

Albert Agueci wa-   Paul Volpe got di-

Juliet "Aunt peg" Anderson began
her Illustrious career in Porn at the
ripe age of 39 an-

"Only the Capone, mob, kills, like

Tha-

The Long Swim to China
(a Left Handed Symphony for the soul of
Tennessee Williams)

1.Nigredo

Was I hatched too soon? & You
Born, too late?

I Consulted the Digital oracle! I consulted, the
Plastic Gypsy.
& yet!

"The
  Haunting question, still-Remains"...

A Smug bastard
Wearing a Black, army hat, & an Ugly,
Vomit coloured sweater, is
Exhaling the scented, Smoke! Of
His suggestively held, "Vape"...
A Mexican drug lord, Escaped from Prison today, using an
Elaborate system
Of underground, tunnels... &
A Self taught violinist, is playing his afflicted heart out
To sooth some, bored, H.I.V
Infected, chimps languishing in a bleak, secretive!
Biomedical laboratories ivory,
Cage.

& yet,
The haunting, hotly debated question, STILL, remains,
& Me!? "ME ??"
I won't answer, it! In, fact, I won't even, TRY,
But-but
Still!! "They" ...inquire.

"In the New Order does the old pattern
Really return on a HIGHER level?"
"Is Carol Cutrere in your Drugstore ?", huh?
"Why do you smoke so much, Lily?"
Wh-
"Why do you go to the movies so Much, Tom?"
"Do you want me to use the Spanish accent, Jack?"
"Does harm seldom befall the wary?"
"What makes you so restless, Donald?"
They ask,
"How doth one stay the very platinum framed
portrait of health in a world
Where even the Doctors may be
Conspiring to keep us, sick?"
"Who put my ice cream in the refrigerator, Stedmond?"
"Are these, grapes washed?"
I can't answer! I can't answer them, Lusty
Babysitters are throwing, caution, to
My gondolas in the – North
Wind?
..East of the black, Lactating

-Sun...

"A large emerald, wildfire raging across Canada
Has contributed to a smoky haze
Lingering above the
Western U.S.A causing a Spectacular,
Red sunset", &
A Known FUGITIVE, hiding, in the most "Obvious"
Disguise, is leading the RCMP, on
An Intense! Low speed, chase....

Was I, hatched Too, soon? & You, You
Born, Too late?

I consulted the Digital oracle, I consulted, the
Plastic Gypsy,
& yet,

That Haunting! 24 million dollar, Earth shattering
Question, still-

...Remains...

2.Albedo

...I have Journeyed far beyond the Salvation of the hair of the MERCIFUL
Dog!
I don't think I'll ever be able to shake
"The Spook!"
I have Journeyed far beyond the Salvation of the hair of the Dog
Tennessee,
My Hands are "Kind of Shaky this Mawnin", My
Hands are "kind of shaky this Mawnin", too!
& The Pharmacy section of the Stage is still Lighted,
Despite the Little pink, & White pills! "Blue sequined Gowns", &
Panama Red,
"This Place aint no cocktail Party!" ... yet? We're
Still in quite abit of "Trouble, HERE, Snakeskin",
& the altitude on this Block has affected My
Golden sphere of a "Ticker",
Too!
It's Still Tough turning yourself inside, out, Man,
Time!
Time Still Lives in this World along with "US",
& Clutches that massive Broomstick it uses, to
Sweep us out of the
Way...
Papa time! that Endless, relentless Idiot Papa Time still has that

Nasty habit of Passing without, Remorse,
The True artist occupies an even
Murkier-
The True artist occupies an even murkier
Position in this Life, than, When You
Were Still with Us in the physical, Tenn,
"Every Kingdom divided against itself is brought, brought
To Desolation", as you knew,
Try being a Poet, Musician, Painter, Comedian, Dancer,
Photographer or Playwright, today,
There's Still a Black goat upon Our un-mown, collective lawn, full,
of white, Crows, &,
Oil Slicked Swans,
Vain Women of Leisure, &
Contemporary, "Epicene Dandies", are all TARTED, up, still, Wait
-ing,
For... Nobody, like a Smouldering, un
Touched cigarette-... Burning! in
An ashtray -
The Sinister billboard sign of a Grinning, fLaShInG Devil!! Is
Still Peeping through our bedroom, & Bathroom windows!
"Enemies of the delicate everywhere have breathed a pestilent mist into
the Air"...
The "No neck monsters" & the stingy, piss elegant daughters of-
Over opinionated Cretins
Our Society has Lon Chaney Senior'd, Leonard
Zelig'd, Frankenstein'd, Patty Hearst'd & Fred C. Dobbs'd are still
Mucking about, conspiring to convert Our Little "Heifers", into!
In-to... "Breaded VEAL"...
& Everyone's "Ravaged Young Face"! Everyone's
"Ravaged Young, Face", May
Be,
THE Face,
"That Tomorrows Sun will Touch without Mercy". I,
 Too,
Have sometimes needed, desperately,
"a Little White ship to Sail the Dangerous Night in",
& Sought in vain that "Cleft in the rock of the World", that

40

Only the Shrinking violets, will eventually Break! In
Which I could,
Hide,
I Myself, am Striving HARD to Recapture
The ability to Say "My God!" instead of Just...
"Oh, Well",
My head has always been buried in the Drooling mouth of
 that "angry old lion", & The Clouds, Tennessee,
& My two left feet! Made out of, Clay,
(If I'm Being honest) have
Scarcely ever been firmly Planted on the
Ground....
I, I, I, I, Too! Have "Tricks in my Pocket", yea, I, I Too!!
Got "Things up my Sleeve"... Will not-
"Will not one fish More", keep the Coywolf, from the feral cat
with Bejeweled Claws amongst pigeons,
Outside Our Gnadiges frauleins, door!? Aquatic, prehistoric Monster
Among angels Fallen, or Elegant Angel fallen amongst "Glorious! Beautiful!
Lovely, transient, black sheep clothed MONSTERS"!! At The end of their
Tether,
Give us Your chilling blessing, Tennessee Williams!
Unloosen your Emerald studded belt!?
Like a "Defrocked priest" at the end of His Rope,
You once proclaimed that
"All good Artists are Monsters in the Sense
Of Departing extravagantly from the Norm"-
& I Agree 110%,
Those who've always been Dearest! Nearest to My palpitating heart,
Were never like those -OTHER- Horses.

Did Your Sister who went mad, Rose, REALLY masturbate, with a Stolen
Altar Candle? Look,
Would you ever've been able to believe that men & Women Would
Have to contend with Rising cancer, rates, & thinning hair,
In 2022/3? Look,
I Don't know exactly How it happened, or WHY? But I Too,
Found myself stumbling through the Meat grinder in that Pain
 Filled, "Dragon Country", Inhabited by the "Flesh

Hungry,
Blood thirsty Ogre" at the Top, of
The Beanstalk, devoid of, HOPE..

"Natural Disasters eliminate Ideology!"
"Infatuation is even Blinder than Love!"
... Cold Supposedly Kills more people than Heat!
Tennessee,
& No Child should ever have to Out live their Parents!!
Am I Right?
Death, Mr. Death is still inexpensive here, Tenn, &
"A Shot Never does a Coke any Harm",
Walking, is now,(Allegedly) the Deadliest way to Commute!
& "Perspiration is... Healthy?"

Let's Not Fight, Sugar, O Tennessee, HONEY,
"Let's Don't Quarrel",
"Please, no whispers around here",
Let's not make a spectacle of ourselves, "Things are
Becoming untenable in my world, Too",
I, I Too, have Identified with a Torn paper Lantern, shielding
A naked bulb, of slowly dimming
Light,
 "A Race horse that's been entered in just ONE race
Too many"
& "A Barely tolerated, financially dehydrated Spinster"
Ill equipped to face the Mysteries of the future, & what Lurked around that
Well known, corner. You
Were bludgeoned, by your own Fame, &
Success!
& Parted ways, (successfully) with the conventions of,
"STAGE PROPRIETY",
You busted open the overly tightened corset of a theatre grown
Stale!
You wrote Novels-
You wrote Novels, Essays, Plays, & Poems that were the very platinum
Framed portrait of your Troubled,
Out crying heart!

You were ridiculed by an Indifferent, messed up, Roving,
Hard nosed Father, who called you,
"Miss Nancy"?
You were Henpecked by your Manipulative, Delusional,
Eloquent! Castrating,
Unaffectionate, "Moderately hysterical"
Mother, & nursed, FUTILE-ly! your Dying,   Ex-lover,
You were Rejected, right when You needed acceptance
The...Most!!
The Critic Walter Kerr once gushed, that
You were "The Man of Our time who comes Closest
To hurling the actual Blood, & Bone of Life
Onto the stage".
You were born upon the same date as My favourite Poet!!
Who Truly, Liked You!
He told Allen Ginsberg that you were suffering
When He met you, in Europe, & "Hung up on Death", &
Were soooooooooo sensitive, He said, like a Raw, "Open Nerve", You were,
He said that He treated you like the Southern gentleman He honestly
Believed You to Be! & You, (Shiva Love you), offered to buy
Him a Return ticket back to the America
He wasn't prepared to face, again, at that particular, time,
Both of You Cats, Shared the Belief that the Artist
& His Work,
Should Be "Inseparable", You & He! Both,
Thought that the Artists Work & Life should be
"One",
You were both weathervanes, like Me! I
 Prayed to His, & your Spirit, like you prayed to the spirit
Of Hart Crane!
Are you both up there Haggling with Hermes, Whitman, Chekhov,
Lorca, Shelley, Nik Beat, Gwendolyn MacEWEN
& Him under the direction of Elia Kazan?
Are you now sitting in the Big, wicker rocking chair
In the Joy Rio in the Sky,
"dreamily munching popcorn" in the lap of God(dess)? With
That Blonde, Blackfoot (or Sioux) Indian, with eyes the color of the
Caribbean,

& an Immense, Drunk rough, impeccably, dressed Sailor, tousling
Your angelic, Hair?
Take me up the steep "Stairs to the Roof" "where its
Cool, & There's
Music, &
They burn that Sweet Poppy",
& The Lobotomized, electro shocked woman, suddenly
Cries out, in Her, Sleep,
I Know the price of Admittance!!!
I won't dare try to side step that "Lavender shawl",
& the transparent, Rapidly falling curtain, of
Blood stained Gauze…torn
Into s/h/r/e/d/s.
I know the price of admittance,
I won't attempt to evade the Inevitable!? Do,
Do you know now the true form of the stone Angel,
Of the dried up fountain known as, "Eternity"
at the End of the Rainbow, Cut into
p,ie.c.e,s? Do
You now know the greedily, hoarded answer,
To the insoluble Riddle of "The Brutal Enigma,
Of Existence?"

When did your Luxurious dream vacation, Morph into
A Life, or Death, Struggle?

& what! Exactly is the Victory, of a Cat! On
a Hot, tin Roof?

3.Citrinitas.

Your "Emotionally biographical" Work, to me, is like an Unrepentant
Stregha, & "Bloddy Teenage Medea",
Burnt at the Stake! on the
Polluted shores, of MOON LAKE-
I Don't care about care Your crush on that "Cruel young gigolo" in Rome, &

44

The Sensitive boy "who hungered for something beyond Reality
& got death by torture at the hands of a
Mob" every genteel "Girl, in the delta set Her
Cap for", or the silver plated syringes you got,
From Dr. Max,
Your works "Truthful intensity of Feeling", to me, was
like a Reformed organ smuggler,
Exonerated,
By the pieces, & The fragments of the youth, of a
Smashed glass, bird-
A Slender, crystal decanter,
"Fragile Mementoes"?
A Terrible, twisted, Delicious, cathartic kind of love... A
Triple exposed, doctored! Sepia toned photograph of,
A Volcanic!
Near sighted Actress appearing
Out of the Immense, Dense fog,
(Of a Binge that Lasted 13, or 14 years) to
Tackle the Highly Coveted
Role...
She'll never be able to   ...Shake,   The
XXX-rays revealing the dark area discovered on
The Punctured Lung, of a Loved One!
A Malignant tumour, found too close to the broken, congenital Heart,
"Rounded like a mountain road"
"The Soft blue dusk of a southern
Spring",
The Chilled incarnate fragrance, of a withered, Barbed!
Formerly lettuce green, laurel, & The Calcinated
Ashes of the tattoo of, a moody, pastel colored, Rose-
A Melted Black candelabrum burning at both ends, held in
The Wayward direction, of the
Cold spot Behind the Exhaustively, detailed, "Brutally exposed", Pain
Stakingly researched, Black, lactating
Sun!
A Clenched Fist, full of "Costume jewelry", Hoisted,
Victoriously, in the stifling, Toxic
Air,

A "Much thumbed" Deck of tarot, Cards, & a STIFF. stiff
Glass of Scotch, resting upon our Bare, Rickety wooden table, "A
Fancily Wrapped, little package", & Something permanent
In a disorienting world of Rapid
 Change, An Old tin, can, tied to the flailing tail, of
An unsatisfied Tiger!!
A Love letter from Lord Byron to a puritanical woman
In Scottsdale, Mississippi,
Our last, wrankled Nerve, TANGLED in a knot-
The dark arm, of a lovesick Beautician, "hanging over the edge of infinity",
Peach colored pajamas of -Rumpled silk, worn by a performing,
safety net less Trapezist!
The Universe as designed with drunken,
& loving vehemence by the... Marquis DeSade,
& "The loveliest Chinese robe you've ever laid
Your blue eyes,
on!"
A Champagne Dinner &
a BATTLE, of Angels " dunked,
...into the Mire"...
The Enormous, emollient
Night-
The Emollient night, has faded into twilight "In the
Winter of Cities"
Of Monuments! In the MARBLE
Oblivion, &
The "Crumbling golden antiquity"... "The
Fiery braille alphabet, of a dissolving economy" ... We're
Skating, still figure skating on thin, Black ice, as
The Spouseless Adriatic mourns her Injured,
Lord, We're
Still sentenced to Solitary confinement! In
Our own, slowly
Shed-ding
Skin,
Your Work gives Voice to something that "I",
& I am Sure,

Countless others have always felt, deeply,
But couldn't quite express,
"No One Wrote for Women! Like you, wrote For
Women!"
No one wrote for FrAzzLeD Pariahs like YOU, wrote
For lost, sensual Pariahs Tennessee,
By speaking nakedly to your soul, I, for some reason
have been emboldened To shed the White blood of my
OWN, onto This Page,
Although, People still do "Horrible things to a Broken,
itinerant Man when he's Unconscious
In the dying, overpriced, hyperkinetic, doom laden,
Blue lotus blossom shaped -city", Although
Something Malevolent might be
Preparing to make its Last stand below it's gLoSsY, ever
Shifting surface, All ISN'T Gloom, "Here",
ALL, isn't, DREAR,   All, Isn't, a
"Threnody of   Despair", to
Create this Poem, I cannibalized Your work! Your oeuvre, Like
You Cannibalized Your OWN
 Life, & the Lives of those around
You, &
Were then, In turn, "cannibalized" by The Demons of The guardians
of The MOON, The Critics! The cri--tics! The guilt, Your
Internal blue, Devils!! & your, own...Muses,
Stripped to their "wine stained rayon" Slips - covering
The water -front...
Although,
The Baying, Vitriolic blood hounds of the chain gang, &
"The Spectre of Lunacy"!!
Are still glued to the expensive heels of Our sweat shop made, Shoes.

"Transparent Animals", Insatiable, Woodland Nymphs,
& Fretful, Emaciated Crones will sink to their Knees "As
If at the Feet of a graceful, Implacable
Deity"...

Alexandra Del Lago & Chance Wayne (smelling of Doom) will
Close the shutters, & put on the
Radio,
& Make believe they are that, pair, of
Romantic young Lovers, facing the firing
squad together, "without any
Shame",
Stanley Kowalski will take off His Silk bowling shirt,
& CLEAR THE TABLE,
As Blanche removes a Rhinestone tiara, & Her cra-cke-d Glasses,
With an Exhausted Laugh,
& Stellaaaaaaaaaaaaaaaaa, will look up, with a Radiant-   smile,
While Brick, Big Daddy, & Maggie the Cat share a Grateful, Much
Needed Drink, with the terminally -drifting,
Mrs. Stone.

The Mariachis & Nightingales will perform off Stage,
& a Penitential Prayer , an increasingly ticking clock,
& an unearthly Calliope , Will be heard...
Don Quixote will bravely raise his lance in a "Formal Gesture", &
Go through the triumphal Arch with,

-Kilroy,
The self inflicted Terror, The Phantasmagoric hangover,
 The Altercation, & The MENDACITY, will, subside! The
" all but complete suppression of any dissident voices"
will STOP! Laura Wingfield's
Long awaited Gentleman caller, will * **Arrive** *,
& the shrinking violets in the mountain will break,
The oppressive, rock, Our........
Tiny, Diametrically opposed Ponds, will one day, conVERGE, into an un
Polluted Ocean that, will, Never end Tennessee,
"The Movement", "The Movement",

"The Movement, will   STILL,   Win". &
The Missing & The

Lost! !

Will
Finally find their, way(s)   "HOME"...

4. Rubedo

"Blow out your candles", Tennessee, Blow- "Blow out your
Candles" with a
Plastic medicine cap between your teeth,
Like a "Purple flower, on a, Red table", &
A sundial made of stone,
"Blow out your Candles"
With no cough to cover the sound.
"Blow out your candles", Tennessee,
Like a ferocious eyed woman, with one of her ankles getting
Bitten by an irate,
Swan,
Or an unscalable, maenad infested mountain, collapsing due to the fall,
The fall, of Heavy
Rain,
"Blow out your candles", with a thermometer
In your mouth, Blow- "Blow out your candles!" Like
A gladiator affrighted by the spectre of
A terrible review, on
Opening night,
Like "ole Bedridden complainers", &
Dazzling,
Implacable young, "shut-ins", Blow! "Blow
Out your candles",
With "a partly bandaged limb",
& a simple invention, that alters EVERYTHING,
As tents are being blown off of their
Moorings-
As a barman slips into his Skimpy "Clothes for a

Summer Hotel",
& impassively WIPES our -dirty- table, to
Raise to a new stage the edifice of modern, Life!
"Blow out your candles", Tennessee,
Like a carnival barker in the French quarter getting
Higher, higher
Than a flightless bird!
& the suicide rate in Japan! On
The newly legal hard
Stuff,
Like "The Witch of Capri", entering a
"Sea full of Medusas" -Like
Two women galloping across a smoky,
Artificial music hall, atop
A mechanical horse,
As if they were an intricate, sand painting done by
A Tibetan monk, Blow! Blow!!
"Blow out your candles", unencumbered by the
Manmade catastrophe-
& the attrition of the knot of papa time!
"Blow out your candles"! From the belly of a BEACHED whale,
From the mouth of a Mustang, Lion, Spacecraft, & Snake!
"Blow out your candles",
"As Mother Earth has shaken many civilizations from her back", &
The stage Is slowly
Dimmed, Blow-"Blow out your candles"....
As a Strange inert figure of someone you
Once cruised at a bar,
Drives out of the dense fog,
In an "Abdicated Roadster", with one of your crushed,
Heroines, to
Deliver, their "Pale Judgement", by
Blowing out your candles,
      Tennessee, with a
SILENT   REVOLVER.

      (Curtain)

Siobhan

A million post punk,
Gothic!
& psychedelic rockers Po
    -go-ing across the
Harsh pink Breeze &
Smeared predominant Yellow, BELLOW
       -ing
"This is what happens to Tyrants!!"
Sacrificed like the drunken Mystics
Teetering on the edge of
The "GO" station platform
     At Union station,
Playing "CHICKEN" with the   Train,
Upon the ecclesiastical altars of
Our Jaundiced eyes,
PUNCHing karmic MILK,
Spil
-ling out of your gloved, Skeletal,
Limp wristed hands
Like the sea Greenest of ALL Bal
    -ding
Glam
Rockers, & Pregnant women
           Smoking?

Neglectful Grandmothers reeking of
Starving Granddaughter,

& Lost ferret being initiated
Into "Something"

That even the most perceptive
Among us can't fully conceive
Of in an intricate, winged!!!
Z shaped structure
On a -Tuesday-
Tender reveries of our Hardest thugs
tReMbLiNg spear piercing
Our Nauseous meadows like a
Blunted needles deflatable SUN eaten
        captain,
Abandoning our sinking

                              S
                      H
                  I
              P
          S...

A stunning! Bulimic girl named
        SIOBHAN,

Cringing at her superb -Reflection,
In a slowly cracking mir-ror,
        Blaring
Patsy Cline's   "Crazy"...While
Snorting a, pale,

K
  I
    S
      S.

a Poem written in Montreal 3

Your Suppliant arms are the life jacket
    I want to wear, to every
        Party.

& On my 2nd day in autumnal
                    Montreal,
      I woke, up, spooning my
          pillow,
imΛGINc-ing, that it WAS

            You.

Whether I was "Lamping" in a quiet cafe in
           Verdun,
        searching my Notebook for an
Idea to bend, REND into a unique,
           Shape, All
        My own, granting Supple, unblemished
        flesh,
To the charred gnawed! Licked skeleton!
         of our inconceivable, childhood Dream(s,)
Getting Roy DeMeo crew'd, By the
       Henchmen,
           Of the house of- Saud, In a
World, stripped,   of the
            "Sacred".

Whether
I was wandering the rain moistened
                    Cobbles of the old
Town, by myself, when every distracted
mind seemed – Stilled-
              Whether I was sauntering! Sashaying
              through! The Mount Royal Cemetery,
The Boulevards saint joseph, & Laurent, or somewhere
                    Off of the hospitable coast of Portugal, or,
          -Maine.

Whether I half heartedly was trying to
                    Halt the hollow
Lemmings, from
              following
A Blind! Wilfully ignorant, man, chasing a pale,
                    Visible
              Phantom over a steep, Muskoka-n,
-Cliff,
In the somber dark, eminence, of the scary
              Living fossil, of Nietzche's "The Last man's
              Utopia".
You were with me, En-GOLDen-ing my Donovan Bailey
Leg'd Holiday
From the "Consensus", Urging, Nudging, prodding
          Me to Slither for
-ward,…Inch,
                         Ahead. & adopt, a fresh,   Ment
                              -ality.

…Your supliant arms, are the Life jacket I "Wanta"
          Wear, to Every-
                    Party.

& On my 2nd
day in autumnal
Montreal,
I
Woke up! Spooning my

..... pillow,   Haydee,

Wish
-ing, It was...

...You.

If that Battery is Dead, IT'LL have Company

Suddenly, Last Summer... Forest Green to the
                    Profession
of -Horse theft.

Wheel footed men lugged their cop stuffed
  Greyhound Bus across the
    Plausible Burial sites, of the yellow &
White, Skies black sand castle of Pelvic- TRUTH
  Being laddled out by the
        generous,
      Resurrected victors of "Life" over Deaths
        Celebrants somber, ethereal white, clad
          Penitents waving olive branches, &,
Palm leaves, & My Glass-VIBE, became
          Bambii's- Mother.

My Porcelain vibe was BAMBII'S- Mother,
"Suddenly, Last Summer". Mot- Mo-

Mottled, dark blue- grey stone, ivory
Sinews, Stiff huge collars of delicate, Beaded lace!
The atmospheric motif of a melted iron bridge
& a computer chip the size of a...
Stamp, Modelled after the exquisite architecture
of the brain of an unwed, indigenous mother, who's recently released
        Sonogram showed us a deceased
        Unborn twin clutching his thriving
        sisters, hand, in the WOMB,
You clashed with riot geared mercenaries & sentient A.I

firing tear gas &, Water canons
         in.

…It hit me, with the disturbing, Enigmatic,
immediate finality of the "Scapegoats of 1666"
              or
when Chinese soldiers crucified Tibetans, & put nails
in their eyes, & lit streaking wild, emerald fires under the charred soles
of their Baked... feet, as a hundred thousand flowers
                    BLOOMED...

         Through a Broken-sound proof menagerie of
         GLASS...
i Viewed the heavy price paid for so called
  "Convenience"
to those who have "Conveniently", made things strategically
         so "Inconvenient",
  for everyone, As your flat screen tv's eyes
Started binge watching,
         ME,
The 26 year old champion of the game
  fixers, screwed a sexy, 78 year old
    woman who oddly resembled a
      teenage boy, sky diving in-to! a
      Hot tub, FULL of -Piranhas!
                    Ohio's train
Derailment's toxic fallout was being compared to
    a "Nuclear winter" & full BLOWN, covered up, eco
    -logical crisis"

Black water drip-ped, from Our leaky faucets,

Toxic mould crawled, up our curved, adobe,
    Load bearing Walls,

An Aggressive CANCER, made a concerted,
  Unsuccessful effort, to wither into PURE, Naked
         ---Spirit,

57

Our alchemical!!! Pillars of Herculean-Strength, Demonstrated
    Wisdom &, Lasting unity next winter,
        & Orange haired cyborgs still pecked people's
      3rd eyes out! with
      Their pointy, elon, gate,d, imaginary
      BEAKS Suddenly,

"Thunder snow" pummelled the GTA Last summer, langorously,
The silicon Valley Bank Collapsed,
& the Philippines, which YOU would only ever visit,
        as a "sex tourist" grappled
      with a, *super typhoon* & I
      Could have, cared … Less!
      Drifting past that distant, lighthouse,
        near
      a curved, resplendent beckoning shore some, where, Where
    John Hinckley jr,
  & Lanette "Squeaky" Fromme,
    Didn't MISS, & You & "I" will never be those familiar,
much awaited,
    Kind Strangers with way hotter siblings still
    Disappearing in Kilarney &,

CANARSIE, with Wheel footed creeps, smuggling
Our Narc stuffed grey hound buses
    Across the Plausible Burial Sites, of
    The Yellow & White, skies Black sand Castle
    of Pelvic -TRUTH
    Break-ing, -Left! At the Stick
    -ING<
    Tipping, Equinoctial Point, of   T
              U
           R
        N
          I
        N
      G,

As all bets were off, THEN, That languorous summer,
                    suddenly!

I witnessed the vivacious, CURVACEOUS beauty, & Vicious pointless
cruelty life
                doles
out, to some of it's purest Children's Health & benevolent, well laid
    ...plans, hopes & Aspirations, with a
                Laugh,
I surveyed the immense Destruction, that , that
relentless, FILICIDAL enemy "Time", has wrought down upon us
            ALL... using
that Mobster
manipulating the dubious
        odds, of
                a Rigged contest/game, who
dresses in drag so that he can eliminate his rivals & NOT,
be properly identified by *Eye witnesses* giving a
Lurid, no holds barred account , of every species real history as
            told to us, by it' so called
LOSERS.

My Glass Vibe again, was
    BAMBII'S ----Mother. Mummified in Bubble
        WRAP...

                & Everything that was once given up as being hope
        -lessly
        Lost!
        got brought- back!! into the loving, Warmth!
        of the Harmonious. Fold
            like Lucifer, with his heavenly, wrathful , juvenile father, being
    Re-united

"Suddenly,   Last   Sum-mer"
                    ...Ah!

Quilombo dos Palmares (for Dandara & Aqualtune & written in Montreal 5)

"The Sky was clear,
The gorgeous weather was Balmy &
                                    Bright.

When the single shot
Muskets, &
Gattling guns mowed us
Down like silver grass
By a purple, man
                    made,
                        Lake.

I recall chemical infused mist, settled...
Over the Conestoga wagon...
Site,
In the intermittent Lull, as
We Fled, & -they-
   ... pursued.

After 12 hours, & 6 uncresting waves,
 of unrelent
-ing, Bullhorn formation,
                    Attacks.

I heard Buck shot was   used, To
Maximize the
"Casualties" ... We

(You & I &,
-Ours-)
Hardly saw the Twilight of
The Break!
        ... of day.

            They said We were
Buried in the blue blood covered, un
-tilled field, of the impaled, 2 miles
from our destroyed villages, where the harvested
wheat was left to
Rot! Like the crystal
Beasts!!
of the Chainsawed, Sleeping
        Walking
                forest.

But that, was a different
                        Time,
In another
        Life. ..

You KNOW, how OUR
  kind,
Managed.
        Alas,

        To get, Ev
            -en....

The Retiree

Back in the era when most people's idea of being
a Tough guy, was someone sporting Bandanas & Baggy
Clothes acting, posturing like, Gangster Rappers,

My Favourite Hustler was this dude named
(His Name has been -omitted-here, to Protect
the Guilty)

He possessed a rare purity amidst squalor,
Bullshit & Decay.
He would fly deceptively under the radar unnoticed
with his Non prescription glasses & dress
Clothes, or preppy sweaters, flannel
Shirt, & Jeans. Lugging around
Novels, Pencils, & a note pad, more importantly,
A Black, "Jansport" backpack, with a
Digital scale, & inventory of always high quality,
Always consistent,   "Supplies".

To the Cops, Thugs, Desert-ifiers of tropical forests
of-RAIN, & everyone, except the Knowledge'd,
Discerning few, He merely appeared to be
a Handsome college (or university) Student aware of the
Hoarded discovery of the stark illuminations of
the Dawn, Enroute to, or from, Class
…He could rarely be caught "Slippin" on a
Main street, He knew all of the back alleys,
Shortcuts! & scarcely populated areas in the city.
You only encountered him when he agreed

to meet up with you. But if him, or any
of the fierce, shield- maidens, Maenads & Unmounted,
Horse women, of the Moons Bright side, he
used as Collectors needed to speak to
You, They always knew how, &   where,
to Find- You...

He refused to talk to anyone on the phone,
& was the 1st person i saw with a cellphone
that had a keypad/board, for typing text messages
& had an old pager & a coded system for it (i won't
dare here reveal) to communicate...

On the streets his name was only spoken in
Hushed whispers or by the mere tugging, on
the lobe of one's left EAR,
He seemed as golden to us as his Dazzling
selection of *Goods*, & conversation
Though His Lungs had long burst, he joked,
"From Huffing HEAVY -Air"... He was
a TRUE gent, who i feel abit weird
talking about to you, Dear Readers, Even
Today.

It was a genuinely a sad day in mine, &
My Squared circle of friends lives, when he announced
(after giving us a few months warning to "Stock up")
That he had managed to save up enough, & reached his
Goal, By Cobbling together enough shekels
to Retire (at the age of ...32 or 3) to disappear
who knows, where? Never to be jailed, shot,
Robbed, or Arrested! Never to be Seen,
Or heard from anyone of his customers who
Still Miss him & His top notch goods, &
All the Memorable, Deathless times & Insights
they Helped us have, to this date, almost 10 or so
Years, later.

(Hustler's name omitted-here- to protect the Guilty)
If you ever read this, I have tried to remain
as vague about you as i could, Your name, is
Only spoken about fondly in hushed whispers
or by the tugging of the left ear still, My Friend.

...Enjoy your retirement/ NEW Life! Irreplaceable-sir,
& If you -can, please feel free to send one of your Old Horse
Women of the Moons Bright side, Maenads, or Shield- Maidens, My
Way?

The Beaded Medallion (a poem written in Montreal 1)

"Love me then, Haydée! Who knows? perhaps your love will make me forget all that I do not wish to remember...one word from you has enlightened me more than twenty years of slow experience; I have but you in the world, Haydée; through you I again take hold on life, through you I shall suffer, through you rejoice." Edmond Dantes aka "The Count of Monte Cristo"

Wherever you happen to be transplanted
  Right NOW, is the Procession at the Grail
    Castle, of the MAIMED
     King,
      & the Focal Point, to which leans like
      a sufi, Mystic! My entire ---

Being...

The Gold Brick   D
               R
             O
               P
               S!!
When we least expect it,
Haydee,
& Nothing, nothing, not all the training
or practice in this world, could
 have prepared Me!
For   You.

In Every life, there is said to
arrive a magical,
Transmogrifying moment, that
"Old yeller"s everything, that ever
Came before
        It,
& Me seeing you again, At that
Wedding, After all these, years,
Was one, of   "Those"...

I can Journey, I can forage!! I can
expedition
From here to Neptune! From New
Zealand, to ...Portugal,
& Never Discover your- Equal!
Haydee (Who I'm
Droolishly in awe,
                of) Haydee,
whose name means   (Censored)

                    In
a suspected Knights Templar
built Church, I,
Bent a pious, Reverent Knee, to
The Black,
Madonna, (While gazing up, at the
Stained glass Windows)
& lit votive candles to the saints
(John, Roch and Anne)for
The Future happiness of you
            who,
Used to play all 88 keys, of
Your piano, "Oblivious",
 to my EVERY
"Hello".

You have recently Be
                    -come (without
even really trying) the Infallible, un
-sniperable Queen
Of ALLLLL
-L,
I survey
To me, you are the Lush En
-forestation of a
Hyperkinetic, Blue lotus blossom
Shaped,
Doom laden city of Liquid, speckled!
Philosophic
Stone,& a Humongous dinosaur
Breaking out of
The cosmic EGG, of a TINY
Bird,
If I was a Terminally ill man,
 you would be, the kept
Promise, Of a NEW
---day, I want!
I want to make a lewd joke, out of your most
cherished, rigidly clutched Beliefs, to loosen
you up, aBIT,
I wa- I want to gift you, a
Soft watch! Glued, eternally, to
 Midnight! I wa- i want to
serve you Feathered Beef & grey, ROASTED, oil slicked swan, On
 a rectangular, plate, decorated, with the
Severed head, of the languid
 afternoon of a,
Faun,
I want us to Become Accruers/ amassers,
                        Haydee I,
I want "Us" to accrue/amass it, ALLLLLL, Together,

If you're willing,
I want us to go THROUGH it
...All,
I want us to absorb "everything",
& through our two Stunning,
Reliquary vessels,
Everythinggggggg, & it's inveigling sister's "living work of
DADA" will find an
Inimitable,
Shining! Soul boggling, Expression! I am
Start!!

-ing to suspect that every good poem
I have ever written,
Despite, whoever it might be dedicated
To,
Was in fact, written for (or about)
          You
...Archaic places, are still PERISHing, into
modernity, Hay
-dee
Our Donovan Bailey, Usain
Bolt Legged summers are still Wilt,
-ing,   into the cringe worthy
              Past,
& everywhere We now
 turn, we are confronted with the
stern Countenances
Of those, who's stale -Destiny! We
would
Rather face the firing squad, & jump, into
 a pit of Punji STICKS, then
even slightly ...resem
-ble...

Stepout! Sally! Forth, Unfold
Hermosa,
 Blossom, break on through, Emerge!
        APPEAR   out of the   dense,
carcinogenic smog,
Disorienting noise & calcinated
- ashes-Even "If", You don't, dig
…Me,   I

See, Saw &,   SEEN, something in,
you, That I never believed
I could ever
"Again", witness…

…Even if our two paths, Never
again, cross

The image of us Dancing, Slow
                -ly,
at that Wedding, To "All my
Life",
will stay with, ME, for the rest,
        of-   Mine.

Golf is Bourgeois, Soccer fans are ANNOYING, & The Toronto Maple leafs suck! (a poem written in Montreal 4)

Houses can WALK! …Walk, Houses can
MOVE,
i'm under- Them.

…There's nothing quite like meandering around you
in the Rain, Montreal, but Right
            Now,
I'm Literally melting within your sweltering Summer
Heat,
My Beloved Grandmother's & Uncle's Cancer, was just diagnosed as
being-Stage
 4-
& I don't know, exactly what direction i am Heading toward
in life, at the Moment,
But am aware, that there is no chance of shelter!
from the Nuclear,
            Oncoming storm, that we are all
Visibly, unprepared for,

                    HERE,

Here,
Contagious Enthusiasm, DEFIED stereotypes, Mended fences & ties,
Cautioned
WIND here, REALIZED potential, & the inauguration of the eternal
season

of perfect-Health, HERE, a claustrophobic man
suffering the delirium tremens at rush
Hour,
aboard a packed, Bus! & "Resurrected Mummies seeking
Vengeance upon the callous archaeologists who invaded
        their Lovers Tomb",
The society of righteous & Harmonious
        Fists,
People who pine for company dining at restaurants,
Alone!

Women who adventure to the movies by them
Selves! Here, Rhythmic talons trimming melancholy
Sepulchres! Here, consoled Bloodless wings, fright
-ening Distant- Marble,
        Attractive!
Lust crazed female teachers stalking their male, students,
& Sending them raunchy selfies, "Sexts" &...
Devastatingly effective, Emojis LOL

Here,
The Counted Blessing, the Lived, dream, RAISED standards,
                Here,
The Dodged Bullets, HERE, are Bridged Gaps &, Answered Prayers Ah!
The THANKED lucky-stars, Walked TALK, gratified
Ambitions(s), fulFILLed
wishes,
CUT-MUSTARD,
Granted Boons! Mass non compliance, Changed
                games, "Here"
GRINDED axes, saved bacon & skin, Conscientious Objection,
Practiced PREACH, Questioned authority-- here, &
Jumped sinking, ships...

The exteriorization of liberating, possibilities,
& the exemplification of the lift me beyond the stars mixture
of blue menstrual, Blood! & Pink
        -semen.

I journeyed here to you! To Lead the hungry ghosts
of Beauty's Allied forces BEYOND the
      Rubicon, Alps, Delaware, Atlantic & Rhine! RHINE! Everythingggggg
I want/
Need, NEED, & will probably never possess,
      are ALREADY,
            Mine
Here, HERE enough Rupees, shekels, Euros, Rubles, Guilders,
Dollars, Bitcoin & yen, to live on,
            Mine!
All of Your Milfs, Gilfs! "Karens" BBWS, Gingers, Spinsters
& TERFS fretting over my health & over all wellbeing
            are MINE!
...Mine! I wa- I want to "Hear bells Ringing, Dams buRSting,
Rockets Exploding here! I! I want all the Billionares soaring
                  up
to Space to end up like Phaethon, Icarus! or the Doomed crew
that Boarded "the Challenger" I, want all parasitic
            Royal Families
to meet the Hilarious! well Deserved fate, of Marie Antoinette & King
Louis XVI Here, I want all golf courses transmogrified into
Ancient Burial Grounds now!
Here, a little Girls weird cool drawing of a merman getting devoured
by a Bodiless shark, Feathered BEEF & a grey -swan, people in
Scuba gear are shooting harpoons
      at...

"Here",
The Gnawed chewed licked sucked hidden skeletons, have been
dragged out of the cramped closet
      a few decades ago & Boldly lobbed! Lovingly, upon
the Breakfast table for Us all now, to SEE, Here, The
Turqiose veil of secrecy, The Coarse,
Silk burgundy curtains they have tried to cower behind,
Have long been ope'd wider then the tracked marked legs, of
Your every ex-boyfriends (or girlfriend or whatevers)
            Mother,

Here,
The Dweebs/ TWERPS,
organizations, Industries, collectives & Cabals, that make life
almost seem (sometimes) not worth living, & make us doubt our
Own Innate Beauty have been REVEALED, here we
Define our Troubled times, Do we
   Not?
Like Brandon Pitts told you in his epic poem
"LOT"
Since this be the case, how
      Now,
Do you choose! To define THEM, Here? Yes,

I know your Beautiful skin is Brown, Yellow!
   Red,
White! & every shade, & admixture
   in,
---Between--- Here,

BUT WHAT COLOR'S YOUR SOUL?

I confess HERE that my first crush was on a Beautiful girl
Named "Helen" who had Orange hair, who was
Half greek, Half irish, who everyone
Bullied, & Nicknamed "Smellen"... I confess!! Here, I haven't
Been to the Dentist since the morning of
Sept.11th, 2001, a Philipino Dentist with her Ample
  Breasts pressed against My
    Severed Head
as She picked at My teeth with Sharp, Metallic
Objects as Her! & Her
Assistant watched The fresh footage looping, on
CNN, Here
  I, Read about the World's Dirtiest man dying shortly
after taking his first Bath in..Decades, &
Can hear "here" the chicken little-ing on social media
   I,

I can see the Milked Tragedies, O Blessed Resurrection,
I can see People whipping gravel, Eggs, & Shoes at Panic
Button carrying Politicians Here
            I!!
Can hear the cold dirges of the Baffled, Militant, *Anxious* & spooked
making snow angels in
The shifting, garbage littered sands
            I!
Can see what the gelatinous, multi headed, thousand
Tentacled scarecrows hovering, lurking over
the tranquil blood coated fields of the
Impaled, are bringing to Bear?
But i refuse to parrot their puzzling, unquestioned Narrative(s),
& Join their retinue here i! Have long tossed away
the Daily papers, & flicked off the mainstream
            News

Here,
My life has started to become a CRUDE parody, of
that movie "The Lost Weekend", Di- Didn't
We beat nearly 100 million other Spermatozoas in a vast race!
to fertilize our Mothers Eggs to be able to -Exist, So
   How can any of us be considered
      LOSERS
            "Here"??????

Here my Beloved Grandmother's & Uncle's Cancer, has been diagnosed
as --Stage 4-- Ther- Th-

There is nothing quite like Meandering around you
In the Rain, Montreal, but right now, I'm
Literally melting,
within your SwelterING summer
      Heat, & now,
            My only Idol, is - ENOCH.

2 for Besha Starkman

1.

I was duped!!
         I tell
             you,
Or My Judgment was
                Impaired!
When I agreed to Come,
    Back!!

To THIS, Planet,
           Unless!
It was to be
 with ...YOU...

Your Recent Tornado, has
           Ripped apart
   My Kansas.
    I Sit,

Entombed in the Toronto Reference
Library,
    Flipping through the
               Journals Of
                   Keith
            Haring,
By a Rain stained Window, Picturing

You,
Bare shouldered, In a Purple
                    Orchard,
Swathed In the unbearable white! Un
            Onion skinning
                    Light,
            of
    The Black, lactating-Sun,
        Cheering
OBNOXIOUS
-ly! ! For a
            Game,
        ..Already
                Over..... A
Peregrine Falcon still shackled to
                A,
Shimmering- fountain-a
                    Conestoga   wa
                        -gon?
                A
60 LEGGED CREATURE!!
Biting into Green
                Onions,
As if they were BLUE apples! Nibbling
                    the Chaste Crumbs of
Delusion?

A Solo… Band!! A,
            Recently awakened Somnambulist
                            Skipping
                    Along
                The
                Cylindrical
        Sands of
    My
        Beach!

That Doesn't, even ….EXIST!
…A White
Elephant caught in a
Hammock?
A Pink Elephant caught in a …..Hammock! A
Sports Star mocking a
                    Disabled girls
"Selfie"! Or,
The insatiable offspring of,
                    ……"The Blob".

I Picture You!!
          Alas, as a Pirate from
The Tropics, Captaining your hole
          Filled, Boat! Across
      My un-navigate-able
          Winter --Sea,
…I envision you as a hundred, Sprinting Shee
                    -ple,
Evolving into a Walking, leafless!
Snow covered Tree, made, out-
Made out
          of Olive SOAKED, Com-bus-tib-le,
      Oak,
Until...

A group of Cackling, University students
Stab a FEW,
            Pins,
In The Water, bed, of my
                  Imaginings,
                  I
Look Out The Rain stained wind
      -ow on the
      4th Floor,
of The Toronto Reference Lib
      -rary,

To catch the sight of Two
                              Planes,
Colliding in Mid,

-Air. ...Our Laurels,
            Are only Forest or lettuce green! for
      a,
      Season...a,
                  Season...

Our previously discovered, Pioneers, are
                                    Gyrating
                  Wholesome
                        -ly
Along the "Uncharted waters"!! Of
      A New

            frontier.

Our Undelivered,
                  PIZZAS!! Contain No
"msg" &,
            NO Added
transfat?

...Like
Le Comte de Saint Germain ... Besha
            Starkman.

Your Spirit Will, NEVER !!! Your
                              Spirit will,
            NE'ER,
Your Spirit Will,
      Never,
            Be a Moustache,
                        Pete.

2.

                                        Never,
Never will One of my nostrils ever know the
Incomparable pleasure of getting clogged, BY
Your Pharmaceutical, grade,
                        Blow, Never! Never
Will you be both the "Virgil", & "Beatrice",
Of My Epic "Inferno", Nor
Can you be My Much needed Jocasta now, no...Never!
                Never
Shall My contemporary Opium dens Peddle
Your Platinum dream Inducing, merch, or Get People
Strung on the Highly pure morphine &, "Ron",
You & Rocco
Pushed across Ontario, & beyond.....ah, Never!
Never will My Lips get a Chance to sip your Diluted,
            Bootlegged
Liquor that would decimate My
"Already" damaged, Liver...
Inside Your 7 door, 16 foot long Marmon,
Touring sedan I will Never get to Clutch Your, Severed,
Prosthetic, Jewel laden, Hand, as
                You
Sit beside me wearing Your Black! Satin dress, Mink
 Coat, &
Wide Brimmed, hat, both of "Our" watches, Eternally
Glued, to- Midnight...Never!! Never will
My golden cross get buried
In your mystic
Rose? You may now be, Where
Six thousand Monarch butterflies, are
Cuddling together on the flimsy Branches, of "Our"
Walking! Leafless! snow
covered, Bird crowned, simian haunted
Tree?
You may now be

where the Insatiable "Psychopaths in- Charge",
The "Tin gods with totalitarian pretensions" & Their
Foot soldiers, their Minions, can never get You,
         NOW,

So where You AT!!! Jungle,
                         Cat? Where are
You? Where art, thou? WHERE,
         Be,
      ...Ye?

I've Checked Under beds! Atop of Skyscrapers,
I browsed "Tinder! "Bumble" "Plenty of Fish"! & "Ok
Cupid",
I even posted ads on "Craig & Leo's list" &, "Kijijii"!
Not to mention
all the City
         Papers,
  I Looked inside of Dreams! Sheds, Caves,
& Burnt Books!
When I was Consorting with Known
Saints! Mystics! Grinders!? 85
                  year old Strippers, "Karens"
                  & Crooks!
I've travelled to Deep, Dark, Inner, & Outer
 Space!
Just to catch a glimpse of your
Seraphic ... face! I
Can't Swim! But I, SWAM, Every
Red, re-parted River, Ocean, & Sea! Just
To see where You may,   BE.
I Crooned purer than Sinatra, Morrison, & Orpheus to You! Under the
Nocturnal nights
Moon,
I Mutilated My young mind as an Offering
To You. & your Auburn
 Hair,
Every Dawn, & Noon!

You said,
You were the Universe's Lavish gift to
                ME,
You said "I" could've Made "it" with,
You,
If I Laboured the, Hardest,
        I Dema-
I Demand You at LEAST, tell me what
Happened to That?

...Do You not Remember
When I read about the exploits of You & Rocco, for the 1st
Time?
You seized My Soul that Night, when In Your historic Bed
You first got ME to,
Climb!!
You have me obsessed with Alchemy! 166 Bay street in
Hamilton,
Compulsive self, Indulgence! "Harmonics" & Gifted
Athletes Spiritually Injured before they
Reached their
            PRIME...

Me
& You! Would have been The Perpetual
"Fish out of water", &
The Eternal Deer in headlights Receiving
A Rejuvenating hand- job, from a
German Tourist who lost Her Arms in a
Suspected
Shark Attack off of the Coast, of
        ...HAWAII,
Me & You, were, were Like a washed up Comedian & a
Suicidally Despondent, Dancer,
who had to
Cling together to find some vain hope, & vague "Meaning",
 in Their disorienting Lives
where Our

Deceptive, unconscionable Truth, Lies! & Necessary evil,
Dies?
Your black, sex reversed Horses, should
 have became, My - Shattered
-Window...
Your morning breath! could have been My STACK of
Used, Books! Your

Over populated Universe, would've Became
My
CONDEMNED, house! Never, Never will
that bleeding moon,
Glowing
Over the Eldorado of My open grave Renew, YOU ..Your
Legend managed to reach out & console this
Poet,
At the beginning of the epoch my Inner compass
Started leading Me -Astray,
Through an
Interdimensional doorway, that opened
Only Briefly in, Time...It
Is Still said "You
Died- "You Died the Way you were
Supposed to,
Die"...In You! My Millennium long, search! Could have found, it's
Long sought, -Conclusion..... Never,
"Daughter of Babylon! Daughter
Of Sodom! Never"
AH! ..Never,
On "This side of Death" NO!! Never
In THIS world, Besha Starkman....Bessie,
Perri,
Will We, EVER!! Have a, chance, to...
                    Meet.

a ripped snapshot, exhibited in an expensive, broken frame (a Basquiat Commission for 2 Friends)

If you Could Live in any Structure
Designed by
      A) Frank Gehry
      B) Francesco Borromini
      C) Howard Roark
      D) Frank Lloyd Wright
      {E) Antoni Gaudi}
      F) Moshe Safdie
     or G) Le Corbusier
Who's structure would you choose
to Inhabit like mussels,
      Clams, & other sheLLfish getting
Cooked alive in
Western Canada's "Poison Oasis" by the ExTREmE!
Devastating Heat←···?

a younG, chameleonic, self destructive KiNg & Regnant QuEEn
 get
Guillotined & SilkscreEneD upon an arrestin-g,
 primed canvas causing
Questions of $$authenticity$$???
Hidden in a warehouse from the wiiiiiiiiiiiiDe, prying eYes of
overprivileged collectors, investors, & GrEEdy, salivating
     …Patrons …tryinG to steal awaY with
   it,
before it even

~~Dries.~~‡to give as an unwanted birthday
  gift,
to a soon to be++++ ex-©love©R.

2 cars (& a 100 Wild, syncretized sTyLeS) colliDE somewhere
near a skeLLy court on the Lower East
side, somehow, sending a panhaNDLinG
    -- transient,
slumbering in Washington Square Park, to
the Hospital where a BrilliaNT,
TrilinGuAL, Burroughs-ian, Creole kid saMPLing, & Re
-MIX-ing a "~~Diseased~~ Culture", doodling a picture of
a gun to mail to Richard M. Nixon, discovers
that his *anatomy* just,
hapPens to bE

~GrAy~
From HERE to EterNitY, &, PricEy, vampiric
---FaMe's ~~EdGe~~
Where we all know what pluraled cowards, will
    give,
to get rid of-youuuuuuuuuuu over "hills of
    Cocaine"
& there is still NOTHING, NO-thinG to be
gained ((*HERE*)) where The spinning World has Rapidly
    ChAnGeD!
But the SAMO© **Shit** still
Occurs/remains & in some -cases, is getting even
WORSE. The Test tube ALWAYS falls, into
Carnivorous hands   While
a Man Dies †Man --DIes ††
Man --Dies ? Man dies !†† MAN
    ~~DIES,~~
MAN DIES† MAN DIes† MaN DiES††
Man- dies!!††
But His Shining →★★☆Legend ★★☆‡
    WON'T/ Ca
      -n't!

...AL JoLsOn Vs Malcolm X?
Hannibal Vs
      ROME!? SocietAL UtOPia veRsUs
ReliGioUs HeavENS!? Jesse Owens, Jack Johnson & Jim ThORpe!
    VersuS J.
Edgar HoOveR? MK-ultra vs...
     COiNteL PrO?!? The Tuskegee experiment(s) vs
 Operations Mockingbird & Sea-Spray!?
ROe VS WaDe, WADE, Anita Bry-ant VS ...
BESSIE sMiTh!? Beetho-
     Beet 🔀
 Beethoven's "Eroica"/3rd symphony - Ravel's "Bolero",
     The
Visual voice(S) of the plumage of a
     NIgeRian
PeaCOck, Assorted Jazz & ALL the music,
     Tesla's Coil "Coulda" ♪played ♪
is BLASTED⟵ BLa ✹ Sted
on repeat in a big Brain picked like
 a fat poCk-Et, or a grEEk ...Salad Though every gesture is
 Symbolic,
~~Abrasive,~~
Incomple...Oddly-BeauTiful, &
 Every poignant actioN, a Fabulous EVENT→
The Increasingly soaring costs of Existing/rent, are still
     Due,
Another SuperstaR athlete gets drained by
the Managers, SpouSeS, Family, leeches,
"Frogmen", & Entourage that
SuRRouNd THEM 🔀

Really old shoes take trolleys for   half
of what was houRs soFt slow...smells
steaming hold uP, in a rentEd bEd & letters,
ThE ColonY of RoAcHeS in the oven still lay eggs
under the tiNfoil in the oiL sWamPs, of
Broiled SteaK cooked, & UN-cOoKed by
"the Laws of Liquid?" & Jimmy best is still on his back

to
the sucker pUNChes, of his ChildhOOd files
& colour, of his splotch covered,
        FLESH 🔃
The DEaTh Of MiChaEl StEwArT
        & Clifford Glover,
~~"THE Death of Michael STEWART"~~↩···
THe DEATH of MICHAEL Stewart still gets re-
created over & over, & over, again,
with only slight variations multiple times a year,
since it happened.
Hollywood Africans in front of the Chinese
                theatre
with footprints of Movie stars,
"The Irony of Negro ~~policemen~~" is even
MORE ironic into todays climate,
& LIFE is EVeN +more> CONFUSING now then it almost
        everrrrrrrr
        rr
        r,

        WAS 🔃 →

Taboo Perceptions, "Colonial (& Impostor) Syndrome",
Everything interrogated, & staLe, outmoDed stereotypes
are being DeFIEd, then DumPed, upon their severed,
                                H
                              E
                            A
                          D
                        S 💀 💀

ImMediate & Dir
 -eCt!
A fresh, RaDicaL Painting to match your. surfed .couch. from "IKeA"

New ART, New MONEY, New
YORK,
New(//NO) 🟡 🟡 🟡 🟡 WAVE!!!

Half Erased, cut up words, Pictures, Dropped names, symbols ⬆ ⬆
Diagrams, References & Facts
scrawled, scRATchEd & LAY-eReD unto tagGed walls,
💣 ✳ BoMbEd 💣 ✳
 Subway !trains! Fashionable clothEs,
Decay
        -ing, intercultural ~~streets~~, repurposed--- WOOD,
valuable DEtRiUs, &
 other discarded ma-m-mater-~~materials~~ in
a RuGG
-eD,
yet precise, uNstoppa-ble, Ocular, passionate ‡‡
            Swing→
Incantations!
            & BOP!!
About ♛ Royalty♛, hEROiSM, The--StrEEts!!   The
~~Streets~~!
Hero-isM, & ~~RoyalTy~~ ♛
                To mAke Us ALL, pay -Attention⬅⋯⬅⋯. for
once???

A
 Series of Drawings & Black & White Xeroxes of
        a Mascot'd,
        alchemical, GIGANTIC celebrity,
(an angry, Janus like,
Exoticized OTHER) who
was "~~Not for Sale~~",
Facing discriMination (& some Believe +Over‡
──────── ~~hype~~+)
being unable to get a single hailed "Taxi
Driver" to hALt for ThEm, after stalkiNg down the
Money littered $$$ cAtwALk $$$$
at a drear fashion show, in the exciting, bankrupted,
fertile!
 Insomniac city of their fruitful, Auspicious
                    ====BiRTH====

Some gossip about his conquests of MADONNA←⋯
OYA, stuffy art world-+ ladies, downtown girls
      (allegedly some Boys/men, too)
      random Models, "Mona Lisa"
          & ~~VENUS,~~
& His 1000$ a day habit to forget his mother
in the MadhouSe,
 & the disapproval of a father
who staBBed him in his aSs, for getting cAughT smoKing

    → POT.

Some Whisper that the mOOdy Man who
conjured "the Self Portrait self portraiT of the aRrtist
as a youNg deRelicT"
 & HEEL Made a Trickster
Bargain with that Deity "EXu/
     EsHu"←⋯

Some SAY! He made that Blues drenched deal
with the breeder of the Hellhounds at the mythological
      ~~Crossing~~
    of the ROADS ††††
gained that Amber, x-ray vision, got the ~~GOLD~~
——————& began
to make the bold decision to Whip Bolts
of ⚡ ⚡ THUNDER ⚡ ⚡ &
Lightning ⚡ ⚡ back! at filiCidal SatURn™, ShAngo™,
& ZEUS ™.
As The Son of Barney Hill Descend
-ed, like a FaLLeN
ANGEL! or the Cadillac Moon's famous Ruler
with ISHTar,
 ×××TO REPEL --GHOSTS.×××←⋯

a NOte wrote by a true Friend in
    -the end-
"I DON'T WANT TO SIT HERE AND WATCH YOU
    DIE," it said

"Another episOde of *Celebrity* DruG AddiCt" cliche.

"I/We Had NOOOOO- Idea" folks

"A) That He was a handsome Junkie
 B) Is still a depressed, halo'd junkie
 C) trying to quit" in Hawaii,
 atteMPting to get ~~sober~~.

SoariNG
…Riding (after doing a spEEdD ball) with ~~Death~~ on the back
of a *Pegasus*,
like a LWA, a blazing ✄– comet ✄–✄ & Ember, an ~~Orisha~~,
        a BIRD
 or an Un-
        snuffable ~~candle~~
          burning
at Both ends in the NOrth-WiNd-" East of ThE
        4 moMents of the
            → 🤢 ☀ SUn" ☁ ⚫ ,
The Indomitable, ToRMeNteD, IconNoclastiC aRtisT critics
        & short sighted ~~Curators~~ claimed got
Locked in His gallerist's/ aRt pimp's Basement in order
to ⚫ crEatE ✳ ,
& LabeLLed a briEf, feather weiGHTted flash ✳ of the spiRit
in the Teflon
PAN
's Name is Now EnshriNed (for all ~~TIME~~), among
Art HIstory's ImMoRtaLs, atop Mount OlyMpuS, Defying
 -Categorization- While copyrighting ©©©DeFACe
-MeNT©©
©

wearing a VerSaCe Suit, one victorious raised arm, grip
        -ping
a drip-piNG brush of
expensive, floreSCeNt painT in
the Air of some- Museum, a PlatiNuM! DiaMond

Encrusted ©crown©
of ~~BLOOD~~, & thorns ♛♛♛
upon his fearless,   Sneering, mAsk covered

S
K
U
L
L,   Starting to--- (LaSt) -LauGh. 💀 💀 💀 💀 💀
   💀 ←···⚓

from His OpEN→ ~~Grave~~ ←···♛.

Where did "Cokey Flo" Brown escape to on the Horse that Crushed the legs of-Cole Porter?

...I decided i had to make my move, into
the virginal Region, beyond
                              "Their" Grasp.

After Our ascent to the Upper
Echelon, Our fated trip, to
                              The TOP.

...After My NARROW escape, in the Aftermath
of the Lavish, Contemporary
Prohibition era Funerals,
                              for the fallen
Good Samaritans &, Vanishing,
                                   Co-operating witnesses

I had to ask, Myself, "Wha- "What're
You still HERE,
              For?
This wasn't the way things were
                                   Supposed to work,
                    Out".

I had promised i'd kill myself, before
"They" ever caught me, having
Nowhere else, to Go,
                    AGAIN...

While successfully figuring out your un-
fathomable Depths,
& ALL the -angles, peering
around every sharp, disappearing corner, with the
Curved Barrel, of my
     Gun,
I could see that Our kind was critically endangered
&, Might
   Soon be, Extinct,
But My OWN greed almost chopped, my
Badly circulated Legs,
     off…
ALMOST, did me IN, for good…

I knew, if i didn't manage to "touch base"
       quick,
I was going to be "OUT" &
     thought

"What the Fuck, are WE Becoming,

Now?"
While Las Vegas, New York! Macau! & Dubai
Slept,
& Florida, & the Caribbean
    - FROZE

As that Fresh World began to
open,

S
 U
 D
  D
  E
   N
   L
    Y?

& I Took care of ALL the Bull
                       Shit,

My OWN, impeccable way, that
Night,
the Final Preparations, were
                     Made.

For Dayne

Some Bruises are too tender to
really touch, & some pains,
are too Deep to Fully
          probe.

"Loved with a Love Beyond all telling,
Missed with a grief beyond all tears,
To the World he was just One,
But to Us, He was all the World" is
what is inscribed on Your tombstone, Best
Buddy, of My squandered
          -Youth.

I have only been visited by your Spirit once,
though you are always loitering Godzilla-ly,
in My mind, Dayne. But dreamt of
You,   twice.

The 1st I had of you, we spoke
in a Lavender tinged white, light infused
minimalistic Dreamscape & you said
          "Goodbye"
hinting that this life isn't "the End", & in
the 2nd one,
 I was Frantically picking spilled
Ecstasy pills & a pale yellow powder out of
the Gummy/sticky black, & white carpet in
the house on the street, we two grew up
on, in Mimico.

You just sat on My parents
sofa watching me in Disapproval with
All Black-eyes, & I, distressed, but
not enough to stop my Embarrassing task,
Cried out "Why aren't you
Saying anything, Man?" "Say SOME
THING, to Me
… Please!?"

& then I woke up to My then Girlfriends
Grating alarm clock, BLARING, Knowing,
i had just received a friendly Warning,
I wasn't ready to heed, on the eve,
i almost got IN, too
                    Deep...

Some Bruises are too tender to really
Touch, or press upon Dayne, Some
Pain, is too-Deep, to fully
Probe.

Every time I get Nervous to perform,
I Dedicate it to, you.
Sometimes when i trotted into Danger,
got too close to that Emerald fire's
FLAME<
& got myself in some trouble, Your name,
was Ariadne's Golden Thread, & My Mantra,
leading me safely through the Wringer,
& Labyrinths of MUD.
Whoever said that "Time Heals all things", was
Full of-

SHIT.

"Would we still be friends if
You (who

got rooked of a chance to greet the
New Millennium, & an opportunity to
Bloom
to a Full Life? & who we ALL got rooked
of getting to have around) was here with us
Today?" Though this world has steadily gotten
worse, more ANNOYING & LESS
Free,
Since you Fused with *the Divine* is something
I have oft wondered about now that
Greys have invaded my hair, & goatee. Ap
--proaching soon, my late
                    --30's...

It's May 5th, 2022, You would've
been turning the Big 4-0
today ... I'm

Sitting cross-legged alone, in the sun,
In front of your grave, at St.john

the Baptist Cemetery, in
Mississauga,
Ontario, Writing you this Short, LONG
over,   due,   Poem,

My "Adonais".

June 24th, 20*$ (a poem written in Montreal 5 inspired by Picasso's "Sleeping woman Meditation")

On My 106th Birthday,
As I sat on the Varnished Ceramic tile
-Floor!! By the gilded Bronze
                Door,
Flying on the contents of My Jewelled, Pearl
Encrusted snuff
Box,
 watching you
                -Sleep,
(Like an over-imaginative child Worrying
about extraterrestrials Big Brother
-ing the
Movements of the oblivious Denizens, of the
                EARTH,
Like lurking, voyeuristic
Creeps!! Or, a Doting! Anxious
Mother)
On a Red Sheeted, queen sized Bed, With a thin, Blue
Duvet, with
One arm slung over your Head!
                Resembling,
Two unarmed, adolescent thugs about to "Attempt" to, Mug,
An "Ultimate Fighter", OR,
… a Shaolin monk,……. Resemb
        -ling!

Resembling An Eradicated! Usurped! Co-opted Pagan
Goddess whose Worshippers are dead, or some Sacred! Headless!
Arthurian angel, without,
Wings,
Who was poisoned by "Green Gold!" Not
        …Lead…

                On June 24th,
           20$:)
        I actually witnessed, the Beached, Whale!
     The
        STRANDED, leviathan, of your
        soul, ASTRA
        -ly,

     "Flee",
I witnessed the EXAAAAAACTTT,
                  Moment … It…
    Successfully…   Broke

      Free.

On the LAM

       Out here, everything
HITS,
      different... Out here, I am given a
  Clean slate, a BLANK.. canvas, &
am blissfully unhindered, by the laughable decoys,
of Race, Religion, Gender &,
                    Caste,
  & Have no one lurking, over my dandruff spotted, cold
 Chip adorned
   Shoulder.   Out here, I am able to stand
    without a - single crutch, let alone
     two,
      While widening my Dilating! Augmented perspective, & can
Finally escape the solitary prison of the person
      I became ...eventually,
with the murky, predatory!! Self serving assistance of the
         Lowest common denominators
            crude,
     Self limitING   soul shrivelliNG
       Stereotypes spoiled
        progeny, trying
to strong arm -US-, into toe-ing their
Parties fine! Bottom dotted
    Line-, & No longer feel the niggling premonit
       -ions,
of Impending   --Doom!
Out HERE, I am not getting programmed,
By the irrational fear of their Boogey
Man's Red, herring Crying

WOLF, or the oft repeated sound bytes of a/THE, controlled
...Narrative,

& have slipped away from the asphyxiating! Jujit
                         -su like
grip, of the strategic, Philanthropic Billionaires ventriloquists
   Cat's paws restrict
   -ions, back THERE, out... Here, seeing everything through,
      Rookie eyes, from an experiential vantage
         point I can witness
            The thick, lush mane of your Black, Lactating sun set
                              betwixt
            The distant ----Cliffs,
Illuminated by the un-onion skinning
                   Light, of the full MOON, during an
         Eclipse
                  & am not, entombed in the stifling, bio printed flesh
                  covered pyramids, of left,
                  Right! ...& Center. Ensorcelled
over HERE, (in
                     Self exile where the Sea Ends, & the
      LAND begins)
I am no longer weighed down
         By what troubled me in the
                         Past,
      & Can (finally) truly

-Breathe.

The Big "C" suite
(for Dawn Pardy, & Morvil Manners)

1.

CANCER- according to the dictionary
is a "Disease caused by an uncontrolled division
of Abnormal cells in a part of the body"
& "a practice or phenomenon perceived to be evil
or destructive & hard to contain or, eradicate".

Cancer's towering sinister, thrusting veiled Imposing figure, lurks
patiently in the cold, fleeting light tinged dark, to
leap out at us like Norman Bates, attired
"Psycho"tically, as his decaying
Mother.

Cancer is a mortifying, fleshy skull cap, with purple
Buffalo horns, & a long forked, trail of feathers
PLUCKED, from a poisoned, wrought iron,
Quadruple headed-Eagle?

Cancer, "the Big C" can be (at least to me) the
Actual terror of a youthful! seeming, elderly man
Sporting a gauze bandage over the gaping
WHITE, hole, where his Prominent nose use
to-be, Cancers felled dense glazed stunted
timber, Squishes our
opulent cathedrals of skinned scaled-ed carcasses &
Cracked, Broiled, gnawed -bones, with its dismal bread &
Circus, act ...grown
STALE...

The Big "C" can be Jack the RIPPER to some < Freddy
Kruger, to others, Candy man, Ed Gein? Roy DeMeo, &
The Abmoniable Dr.Phibes, to
Me!

Cancer is the CIA, S.A & S.S, & Purdue Pharma, "The Blob",
Dracula & the Borg, Karla Homolka, Moloch , Hiroshima,
Guernica & the Predator all rolled
up into One, BLOATED! Expansion minded monster sucking,
Slurping! & Deep throating our
vitality & fattening itself, upon our delectable Joys,
Plans, Vices, Energy…Dreams, & Love, while trying to
 obscenely, triple penetrate Our lives
PUREST, shadow BANNED children! making snow
Angels in my poems, shifting! Black, garbage
Littered SAND.

2.

Alright,
I was born & delivered via Stork on St. Jean
Baptiste day,
Fors Fortuna, & the festival of
the Burning of the Lamps… The Nativity of
St.John the Baptist … In Eastern Astrology,
My sign is "The Pig", But in its western
Guise,
I'm a "-Gemini Cancer
Cusp" or, simply, a…
"CANCER".

3.

"Cancer-causing chemicals were found in 87%, of household objects tested
in a new
study at
       U of T".

Cigarettes possess WARNING labels on them because
 they cause CANCER,right? the
            BIG "C",
Now there is talk about placing them upon
             bottles,
Cans, & Boxes of- Booze but, By that
    Logic,
Should not we now then be placing them upon
Everything ELSE, we now know ALSO, causes
CANCER, too?
...should not we
Now place labels on Sugar (in it's various types),
& Artificial Sweeteners
Additives, PROCESSED foods, Sunflower,Canola, Soybean,
 Vegetable , PALM & "Hydrogenated" oil, & MOST cereals marketed
    toward
            KIDS,
FAST ...Food, Candy, Chips! Pop ...Pesticides, even more, no?
    Margarine? certain brands of Soaps, shampoos & Deodorant?
Should we now place labels of WARNING, upon
Gas, Plastics, GMOS, Rubber,
Tanning Beds & Sunscreens with Benzene,now?
Place them on or around Construction sites, & everywhere
We Breathe toxins in Our Air, Most sections in Super
Markets, & where ever shines
The Replenishing Rays of- THE SUN?
All the Myriad screens & soul (& Muse) crushing
Jobs & other mindless frivolity that Hamstring People from
Actually getting their asses UP & being,
            ACTIVE?
Since Obesity, Terrible eating habits & a general, over all
Lack! of Physical activity can Cause the Big
      "C"?
Should not we now place
warning labels on ANYTHING that summons
"STRESS", which is well known , to
be a Murderer, & Causes, yes,

CANCER ... The Big

"C".

3.

Look,
The USA declared a national war on
CANCER in 1971, & stated that "they were
close to having it BEAT", &yet,
& yet, after ALL the Money & awareness RAISED,
All the Ribbons & thick, 70's November, Moustaches WORN,
All the rides ridden, & Marathons & races, Ran,
The world as of yet has not gotten a chance
to unite over the big "C"'s defeat, & be in an extended state
of jubilation
at it's ecstatic funeral requiem procession
& MASS,
In fact, "As Vice President, in 2016, Joe Biden led the Cancer Moonshot
with the mission to accelerate the rate of progress against cancer" &
the U.K announced war upon it,
last year, in 2022, since various kinds of,
Cancer,
appear to be on the RISE, despite what some say!!
& everyone knows now someone who has been Victimized &
groped, unconsenting-ly, by IT,

Di- Did you know Cancer was found in Dinosaurs,
& was depicted in Ancient Egypt's
Papyrus?

Ah, Who is to Blame for all of this Misery? is it Not alleviated
because "they" don't make money, from people being
HEALTHY?

Who is to BLAME!!!?

was it god(dess)? or Lucifer? Was it the DEMIURGE?
The Watchers?
was it Adam & Eve & Lilith, &...Steve?
Did it come from DEEP SPACE via Aliens or crash
    -ing comets?
Was it the 1st Barons of Sugar who ushered us by piggy back into Cancer's
Bleak Kingdom?
or should we point our fingers at the prototypical Carnivores riding side saddle
    on
the broken back of cancers skeletal, Brown! sex reversed
Horse, BACKwards?
We will probably never discover the real answer, but
Where's THE CURE they, erroneously say!
Contains No money though towards a cure went,
trillions ? & toward it, more would

Continue to Flow. O!

Is the very source of all this Suffering Mother Earth,
herself? Releasing something upon
Her short sighted, destructive children to show
Us a mirror image of what we did & DO, to
Her?
& how we've spread, Metastasized devastatingly, throughout
& across her without remorse as a Troubled, FAILED Species Way
before we were even dumb enough to have dropped
"Nukes" in her Oceans, Islands, Deserts,
Jungles, Suburbs, Cities & SEAS?
If she is indeed to Blame, Then
None of US, are truly "Safe"!
Because, If her Frankenstein (or ours) has claimed
 the lives of the GREAT,
Duke Ellington, & Billy Strayhorn,
Ralph Ellison,
Gypsy Rose,
Dizzy Gillespie,
David Bowie!

Syd Barrett, & John Coltrane,
Babe Ruth!

If it has claimed the fruitful, illustrious lives of
Gregory Corso, Allen Ginsberg,
ANN SHERIDAN,
Rob Miskimmin,
Donna Summer!
& Russell Means, Dr. Seuss!!
John Trudell, Sweet Catherine of Aragon, &
ChadWICK Boseman! Eva
Peron..

If Cancer's dark gossip has claimed
Johnny & Tommy Ramone, Sterling Morrison,
Chick Correa, Roger Maris,
NIna Simone, Gilda Radnor &, George
Melies,
& Of course, Billions of other beautiful people
Who's names are known only to their
Friends! Family, co-workers, associates, & Lovers,
though out the AGES, then sadly it seems
it could be "curtains" for all of US!
& No one is immune, though it does Appear
as if the vampires & ENEMIES, of Humankind
Don't get claimed by it as Much, right?
What i ask is on THEIR plates? & where
do THEIR chefs source THEIR …foods?
Who are the vatican's farmers? Why,
Why do Popes get to live so long, is that fair!?
& why are Dick Cheney, Rupert Murdoch, Henry
Kissinger. Klaus Schwab, Bill Gates, Anthony Fauci, Mr.Burns & others like
them un-CANCERED?
is THAT fair?
Why did Prince Philip, Aribert Heim, Chairman
Mao, George H.W Bush, & Jimmy
Saville, get to live so long when
So many Benefactors, & Lifts to the species threads,

get snipped too, short?
With all the money & awareness raised, All the marathons, &
 Races Ran, all the Rides RID
-DEN,,
Ribbons & Moustaches WORN,
& Lives affected, I ask again,
WHERE'S The modern Nikola Tesla of its CURE?
I have always been a total wuss around
       Needles,
used to Dread them (still kind of do) when a kid, & embarrassingly,used to
cry lol , but i can
Laugh about it, NOW
& I Never fully bought into the whole covid-19,
        Hysteria...
& i have had the seasonal flu 2 dozen times or more
in Life so far,
So I will never get a shot for those,
But to prevent an arduous, prolonged battle with
CANCER, or fully eradicate this Monster, I would indeed be willing,
to Roll UP

        My Sleeve(s)

4.

Dude!
Are the Dire Statistics (1 in 2) True?

Is it all Just a rigged game of Chance? A cold
Roll of the 18 sided
DICE?
or chalk it up to Dark genetic Inheritance/
       Disposition?

Where are the Cassius's & Brutus's to curtail
Cancer's Caesarship? Who is the Scientist or Doctor who
will be the Magic bullet(s) to It's ...
JFK?

Cancer,

Cancer's dropped penny & other shoe says it will NEVER refer to one single
person as "PLURAL" nearing the palliative light at
the tunnels end lol
Cancer knows that there are 3 sides (at least) to Every story?
& can show that YOUR spoken, individual TRUTH isn't
necessarily THE raw, NAKED , TRUTH in all of it's
obscene, XXX-rated
glory that
Doesn't care about Our
"Feelings".

...Some Children & a few of the healthiest people we know (devoid
of ANY vices) get the big "C" or get
"Heart attack"ed at a youngish age, while
Some of THE vilest, unhealthiest bastards!
  Survive to a ripe old...
Age.

My girlfriend told me that as Beautiful, Bespectacled, over
 looked little girl collecting
aztec tears, living
In New Mexico singing along, in a
Raspy voice to Leonard Cohen's
"Everybody Knows" ... She used to pray
to the old fusia shirted man peering at
Us through the puncture in the ozone
Layer, that there be NO twisters
or the Collective unconsciously summoned
Outbreak, of Nuclear
           WAR...
Well, just the other Night, Hungover, fetus'd
in your queen sized bed my lower lip Quivering
Like Judy Garland's did in "Wizard of
Oz", i prayed
 to MY lost saints because i was spooked,
 about Loved ones maybe developing CANCER, as well
as ...myself...

Some Hypochondriacs of whom i sometimes
am one OF, go to the doctors as much as
Possible, because
they fear CANCER'S   reaching, perverted, Asphyxiating
Hand! trembling at the prospect of the Lowered BOOM of
It's Rhetoric of
"MANIFEST DESTINY"! It's
Fetid,

       "DOCTRINE of --- Discovery"...

5.

CANCER< "Fuck CANCER",
Cancer invaded the ovaries, cervixes, & Skin
of Your Sisters, Lovers & Friends,
Insinuated itself into your deceased Room
mates Bladder!
       Kidneys,
       Pancreas,
       Stomach
       & Blood! CANCER, Besieged your
grandfathers -Throat! Bones , prostate
       & Brain!
Cancer, Accosted Your Brothers, Idols & Dads
Livers &, Lungs! & gave your children "HPV, & Leukemia!
ORAL CANCER,
took the ever flapping jaw of the Pharmaceutical
Grade coke insufflating Sigmund Freud, who kept
right on chain-smoking BEYOND the bitter-end
       Cancer,
       CANCER,
The Man unjustifiably Labelled "DR.DEATH", Jack
Kevorkian, himself, died due to Complications
of...CANCER<

Cancer,
took away 2 of my Great Aunts, Also My

Stepmothers FATHER ,last year! Cancer,
Tried to snatch away the earthly vessel
of the Man I consider to be a 3rd father, to me! But
He Battled IT, BATTERED it, & is still managing
to Party almost Harder! than Ever,
      TODAY.
Cancer, isn't exactly a death sentence today as once it was.

The TANGIBLE threat of Cancer's vicious
RAPACIOUS, ostentatious, solidified shadow borrowed

to Keep!! a few of your ancestors-- **breath,** &
Stole My mothers Gall bladder, ... Breasts, & etc
& Is now in the process of attempting to rob her
& Our family of HER Mother , 3 toronto artists &, MY,
Uncle....

Our alchemical PILLARS of , Herculean

"Strength".

6.

As Mentioned earlier, Human beings aren't the
Only creatures affected by
      CANCER,
Cancers frightening, 6 headed sleazy smirking face painted,
with LIGHTNING, can attack even your rescue cat, & 1 in 4
Cancer detecting DOGS, Cancer affects
even Shellfish, Mice! Reptiles sea lions & Birds!
& in some extremely, rare cases, Whales &,
ELEPHANTS.

Cancer,
...CANCER makes me not squander the gifts given to me
(however paltry) like freckled comely, pale ginger girls

who dye their gorgeous orange, hair... blonde.
Cancer wants to prevent us from heralding the coming
of "the new Young Spring'!
halt us all from becoming "Flighty fortune's Favoured
Knaves"

CANCER,
     Cancer spreading like Artificial intelligence
during the 4th industrial Revolution helps me STRANGLE
     out & SAVOR, Relish
all the ineffable fleeting intra-uterine joy of the present as
       if
     i was a wino sipping some, RARE vintage.
Cancer!
Cancer's serious threat teaches me
not to procrastinate, or take
     anyone i hold dear, for granted,
attempting to beautify all i stumble
     across
& has me hitting, almost daily, the gym, eating
Alkaloids & Gulping infinite
Veggie, Plant, & fruit smoothies, drinking as little booze as i
...Can!

The Big C,
CANCER, makes me appreciate this fucked up
     Life, & everyday, all the time i get
Now to LIVE< yes, Dear Readers,
Alas,
Your Former Baudelarian fatalist, has been
Scared, Straight!
& VIOLENTLY   Converted....

I wish You & all of Yours,
     Health, fun, TRIUMPH
& Love, Blessed

> Long, by the order of Our
> Lady,
>   of the Good
>   DEATH.

    XO OOX...X.

7. the Epilogue

I will Never "Not" be MAD, with the
Way things turned out, & When,
&... How!

If anyone could have kicked its ass, I
Honestly Believed it would
have been,
HIM,
(or my Grandma)

I would have felt completely "safe", walking
Through Hell, & War! With My Uncle,
By My side.

The last few brutal months seem Like being stuck
In Nine Inch Nails' Video for the Song "Burn",
When I was alerted to the stark news of the
Diagnosis, though spooked, I
thought, he's "Got
THIS", as did we
All,
Especially in these puzzling, enraging
Times, When we need him with, Us!
The MOST.

I truly thought, that if anything, he
would be reading something at MY Celebration

of Life/ Funeral service one day,
Not me, at   His…

He was Our inimitable Alchemist, & Brilliant!!!!
Guide out of the dismal, Matrix, &
Muddy, Labyrinth, of
DUSTY MIRRORS,
He was a connector, Our PLUG …The MAN…

Our poignant Prayers seeming fell, upon
Deaf (or Indifferent) Ears, Our Positive thinking,
ended in hot… Tears, & Our Hopes, & vivid,
Benevolent, Unitive Dreams got
        -Shattered
As The Encroaching, Bitter night time
F
A
L
L
S…
As the Sleek, Famished Tigers, were just! About
to Be released for good, from out of the
The cramped cage, of THAT tiny, flightless
…Bird

I'm happy he is no longer in Pain, & it
Must have been Great for him (one
of the toughest people I will ever know) to
Ask to be "Let
…Go". While the Enemies & Vampires,
of Our Species THRIVE.

I will never not be Pissed seeing Robust
Hero(ine)s skeletonized! into
the Calcinated, "Endlessly missed" Ashes
in an Urn, "Warning" us ALL, of the
Avalanche(s) to- come, Singing us the Payed

Piper
  at Dawn's Pearly gates', FACED music...

My entire Approach to ART, has been
Altered,
My understanding of "Life" itself, has been
Shaken,
My community gardens & magical theatres got Contorted,
into more
Obnoxious Golf Courses, Sakk's fifth avenues, & pricey,
Micro sized Condos, everywhere! My already
Butchered, Sleepwalking Forests of replenishing,
RAIN

...Chainsawed, SO open up
More Bio Weapon labs! & Poison the Oceans,
Poison the
Seas, Lakes, Rivers, Streams, Tap water &
every Oasis/Paradise, For all i care now,
Unleash "Captain Trips" from Stephen
King's "the Stand"!!!
"Oppenheimer" the Fractured, digitized Globe
Flattened, but it's Dumbed down, violent,
Youth-anized
Inhabitants (garrotted & sawed in ha-lf) in cashless, concrete
Deserts of Food LET, Hyperkinetic Tent
Cities RISE, &
sentient, Cybernetic Machines pay the Soaring
RENT, As Aliens
Arrive, & Emerald, wildfires streak!
Let Twerps resurrect the ...Bowl/mushroom Cut &
Mullet!!! for
some reason, if they want,

to.

We all got RIPPED off, by this plot twist,
It's Okay to be mad, We lost

One! If Not THE, best of
"US",
a REAL lantern, in the Plato-esque Cave(s)
I will never, encounter anyone even remotely
 like him who, the
Overpopulated Universe seems, Empty
…Hollow, without.

I Will never not be sad, about the
way things worked out, & when,
& …How, Like I said,

If anyone could have kicked Cancer's
Fucking Ass, & escape "the inevitable", I genuinely
believed it would have been, My
Uncle

I can never, will never say "Goodbye", So it
will only ALWAYS , Be a "See YOU

Tomorrow".

August 7th, 2022

Last week,
I spotted Your Doppelgänger sitting on a train from Sintra to Lisbon,
But She wasn't the you who ditched me high & Dry, Before
Skipping off with Some Safe, cheesy, generic Dweeb with a cushy
Bank, job.

No, no, She wasn't, the You who unified my above & below, & then widened,
their Divi-sion, United & pointed all of history's Revolts, into
ONE, harmonious Direction & acted like a Roosted, Compassion
-ate Chicken, keeping a scared kitten safe & warm, during
a Winter storm, in …Texas.

Ah, She Couldn't, be the You who framed, for me, a lurid portrait
of You & the beyond Dali-esque-ness of Life's -Big Picture, Our
Shared! Common, universal Fate…

She was not, the You who, used to admonish me, about how
If I "have an Absinthe or two for your Breakfast,
You'll probably be TOAST, before
                                        Brunch".

She possessed none of Your Erotic Kitsch, & Cold Jollity!
None, of your Ludicrous, signatures of -time, No,
Her Mata Hari would probably never blow lascivious french
Kisses, to the throbbing members of my Firing-Squad, about
to SHOOT.

She wasn't exactly you, but o how she Looks exactly like YOU, gestures,
Demeanor & all… Percy Shelley crossed paths, with HIS Doppelgänger

before his tragic death & it asked him "How long do you mean
to be Content?" But after spending years trying to strong arm
your image out of my mind, I stumbled across, yours!

She wasn't, no, She's from Portugal, so she couldn't be the you, who
helped me count all the ecstasy pills I had in the
Early 2000's, the one who used to stir all of our Mixed drinks, with my first,
Last! & hopefully, ONLY gun.

 Nah, She wasn't the you who last time we met up, together,
I had sex with in the alley behind that bar
in Kensington Market & then, made love with on the roof
of Your Condo near the Imperial Pub,
The Blue Moon light upon us, that WHITE…Night.

Alright, Long, complex story simplified & short, I saw your
Doppelgänger gazing at me on a train from Sintra to Lisbon last week,
& after thinking about everything Listed above,
She came & sat beside me when I returned her gaze, she asked me
what i was doing that night, & …after a few Passionate,
Unbelievable days together, She's sexy, smart, open souled,
Kind, Artistic! We got a lot in common, but she's already hipped me to a
few things like Project bluebird,
 Gabriel,
Sunshine,
& 112, Operation Ajax, Majestic,
Paperclip,
Sea spray,
Big itch,
Mockingbird & Northwoods! (Look them up) The Assassinations of
          Lumumba, Mossaddegh, **Shireen Abu Akleh,** Yitzak Rabin, etc. &
the aftermath.
She hipped me to tthe experiments in Guatemala
               & at,
Tuskegee. The manipulative campaign of the effeminate Misogynist,
Who's shitty, overpriced tattoos tell frightening, soothing tales,
of the Bright future…
She's spooning me

now in my air B'N'B in the Alfama, i got a big tumbler of
Port,
in My Skeletal, Well moisturized hand, & Tomorrow,
We are splitting for Porto, as a new couple,

For the First time, in a long, long while, I am totally excited, to
view, what the Winsome Future, Extends.

weird, how things work out, huh?
Especially after all of the Murky, flakey Bull SHIT, You
Put me, Through.

Simone Mareuil/ Butch Cassidy
didn't die in ...Bolivia

...Every morn now, I rise around about 8am to gull
                    Squawk,
Rumblings of delivery
                    Truck,
                        The Shrill bickering of
the interestingly attired wives of
                        Fishermen, Annoying dog bark,
Vacationing locals, Grating!
Collicky child
            screech, &
                    Big Surfed
Waves smashing! CRASH-ing upon the smooth, Iberian
                    Sand.
Big tumbler of Port in my skeletal, well moisturized
Hand where Celts, Crusaders, Visigoths,
Templars, Moors, Phoenicians, &
                    More   Dwelt!
In a Place older than the Barbarous empire, of
- Rome,   getting
Spooned by the Golden, lady, of My Dreams,
                        knowing
Love, Magic! Romance, Adventure & all of their iLK, still
    EXIST,
Loving the Carnation Revolution, Troubled (slightly) by (location
        censored's) colonial history,
& the dark fate of their Fugitive
            Slaves -Mocambos- I wish had

WON... grateful,
Thank
    FUL
to have been able to escape the Beaded,
Price gouging, Hyperkinetic   city,

        We Begrudgingly called
                "Home".

  So Dip,   DIP
deep into the Medicine Bag, Please fill UP your
      Cup(s),
& take a breath of Fresh, Un-taintable
                AIR,
I promise you, that the Best
        (or most *interesting* parts) are yet to
           Come,
Plummet, Or SOAR, Dear reader(s),
        Onwards upwards & yes,
   Sideways,

       EN AVANT, My

Friend(s), Alas, WE've made

     "IT!"

 ...Cheers.

Beached Whales 4 (6 months later, Back in Toronto) inspired By a Gregory Corso poem & a section Of Kerouac's "Desolation Angels"

On hot December days
She would be liveried in a Nun's Habit,
I'd Don a Priest costume & Roman
Purple
Cape,
& We'd have wild,
Unrestrained conversations
   In his cluttered kitchen,
& Sprawl by the grey ROASTED Swan Haunted
Sea, & Shout!
"*!%^{}[]##????XX???/X//:;\^^--+=$$*6@^
⌐=0()+$$``¬+-t!??X-+= {}*!%??^
@#$%^*&()_-+=":><><}{+ +_)(*&^%^%$#@!~~```~":"><>}{
%tX+$!!?X}{^$@$#)()(?"
    & we would take the Subway downtown
& swim through the endless sea of souls on
    those snowless
   streets!
Staging verbal duels...
She would instigate EVERYTHING,
By drawing first blood,
Casting the first stone on the steep, rickety
steps
Of "The Madman theatre" by saying something totally
Unexpected, Like!:

121

" Che-
Chewing my Aspartame free gum
   Like a Tender Bloody
       Cow
    on the Desired streetcar
      after
Accomplishing the *alleged*
    -Impossible-
& successfully evading, the accepted
      -inevitable-
After helping hog tie up & toss
  a Venezulean Gangster
     into the
   shark, & jellyfish
     infested Ocean
with a plus sized model putting
  -Gorilla Glue-
upon random toilet seats of
     Public
washrooms across Montreal,
  & all around the
    GTA.
After Pawning My meticulously
 Collected -treasures-
    Casting
My Black! Misshapen pearls
   & ethical,
Lab Grown Diamonds of
   BLOOD,
before the myriad, leering
    Eyes
of more then a FEW Obscene, un
    seemly,
   putrefying Swine,
 just to barely survive the
Picket lined, Malignant, Dark
    Aged
Cities Emerald fire ravaged

     MAUI!
We are all in the process of
  being Swan Song'd
     Out of on a sailed,
       Looted,
Hole stuffed ship, of Heavy
        Stone"

& as we would stroll up Bathurst Street
Passing college, I would strike back
      with,
 "I crawl upon your mustard Yellow
Divan
at your X-mas party amongst indigenous people having
a heated debate about Buffy Sainte Marie being
a -pre-tendian- & i, for some reason
feel impelled to tell them all about the eternal glories,
The very historical awesomeness of the father of Canada,
Sir John A Macdonald lol
the delicate sexy magic of his very being,
& am surprised no one attempts to punch me
in my Severed
Head!!!
I make the rabbis Daughters & wife become
Adoring, Liberated SHIKSAS in my king
sized Bed I have Devout, Stuck up
Muslim Girls drinking Pernod, & snorting
Ketamine mixed with abit of Blow as we order pepperoni
PIZZA,
I got Orthodox Catholic Gilfs using Crucifixes on
themselves like Linda Blair Did in the 1st
installment of -The Exorcist-under the
Stained glass windows
of an Opulent Cathedral! After they procure us some tickets
to attend China's Fulin regions Festival of, Dog…Meat!?
& Have Scientology Moms (charred,
Ridiculed, Feathered & tarred beyond
Recognition &-- belief) Spitting on ripped portraits, of

L.Ron Hubbard, on a busy L.A ...
                              Street"

&-
& approaching the ghost of the Old "Sonic Boom",
& "Honest Ed's", she'd reply with
" I WAS BORN IN A GRAVEYARD!
            & I'm
Going to get Buried in Your Hospital,
Because for me, You are
The Last of the MANY! & One, of
    The Elect, FEW, We-
        We are complementary Souls
trapped in the Concept of -Infinity-with
    No way Out, EVER...maybe? We-
            We
are before A! eh? & after, -Z-
 we always WERE, were! &,
    Might SOON be,
        Extinct!
You Occasionally annoy me & you're abit
  of a Mercenary that makes me
want to Scream at you as if i were
        Sam Kinison!!!
            but i think
your grim, collectively Punished Civilians are
        very
    Beautiful/ Hot as
    -Fuck-& I am
Intensely drawn to Your Jolly Ferocity, despite
            my
        ...Better judgement
            LOL
Your Deficient attention,
        & quizzical
Lack of affection toward me,
        makes Me
transmogrify myself into

DARTH VADER,
-The Phantom of the Opera-
        GOLEM
            or
some kind of sith Lord doing
a Fred Astaire, Sky Masterson
        Dance
Number to the Horrible Music wailed
By Nero & CO Fiddling together as
various Bad parodies
    of ROME burn!
Even as I'm twisting, turn
-ing, Dancing! & Churn
            -ing
Within Hell's Hottest!!
  Emerald, Streaking
      FLAME<
The only sound that will ever
  come BELLOW-ing outta my
    Hermetically Sealed
        Mouth, will
Be your Hidden, Un-pronouncable
        Name"

& I, stunned, & semi stoned ....on life?
Not knowing how to respond,
In "BMV" on Bloor street west, She
Would sip her spiked soda,
That was imprisoned in a plastic
Bottle, As I Would yell:
"It was around Dusk sometime that
Autumn,
& the bird races had JUST-begun,
                A successful revolution of the elevated
                    Spirit,
Trojan horsed itself as a lewd Breathing
Living Musical theatre, production,
Where New York, Las Vegas! Macau, &

Dubai
Slept, & California & the Caribbean- FROZE,
& the desiccated, DeBEAKed, Long
Awaited Chickens of Human
                    -Kind,
                Came Home to ROOST
                ...a GIant hand in the -Psychedlicatessen-
                in the Sky kept spilling me, from a
Cracked jar, all over our beaded, hyperkinetic
Dark aged city of liquid, speckled! Philosophic
Stone,
It was one of the turning points of
My life!
I ain't ever seen ANYTHING like, IT
...In all my Born days, Honest-
                            ly!"

& then she would smoothly slide
The emptied bottle back into her bag!
As we would be being ushered out of the store,
Knowing that her back
Was against the ropes,Now,
By the time we were near St.George subway station,
Cyclists, Ubers, Xmas shoppers,etc passing by,
The gloves were definitely off,
& She would loudly, WHIS-per!
                "It was like Genuine, undeniable Magic, un
                -mitigated, in
                 Scope, Scale & Complexity beyond
                all computation! Speculation! Alphabets,
                Nihilism & MATH,
                or sailing upon a Steep,
                 maenad infested mountain of...
                Noctilucent cloud
                 A Naked, Singapore caned man
                was dragged by 6
                indivisible, Enigmatic Lionesses painted
                bright,

refrigerator white along the shifting,
Black! Garbage
Littered Sands to a wet, glistening road coated
With pink--packing snow.   We felt just
 Like we
were only Loose threads woven, into a vast
 Sweater floating through an inscrutable, expanding
 Cosmos/Space & turbulent wAvES, of,
BLUE COTTON, right?"

& she would always remove her
5 or 6-D glasses,
But I'd Keep mine on!
& finish her off with an attack
Along the lines of-
   " Yeah, ok,
The Lemon Blossoms started to
       BLOOM again,
Staunch Free SPeech warriors developed
into delicate, annoying evaporating little
Snow flakes because people disagreed
with THEIR heavily biased
 views,
& the peerless daughters of an
Un-assassinated caesar
                    Ninja
   Kicking Handsome men
     (who Dance fight)
                -FUGLY-
Smoking the highly cherished! MUCH
   Bogart'd Remnants of
 Everybody ELSE'S Joint,
Appeared out of thin air like
       Obese,
wasps invading
  Your picnics in High & Central
       Park,
While Your Stern (yet Beaming) visage

-HATE watched- me from the
        Smog Smothered,
            Euthanized,
Mysteriously grid patterned
            Sky, as one of my
            nieces (who are terrified of Terry Fox) put
polysporin & Liquid, Soap,
    upon
            The Tooth Brushes of your Sister &,

MINE".

(to be Continued...)

Acknowledgements

I would like to Thank
Lori, Dawn, Spencer, Wendy & Samantha Pardy,
Merlin,Amanda, Sean, Aaron, Carlie, Stedmond, Morvil, Warren, Martin,
Meghan, Warrick, Amanda, Malik, Juliette, Hannah, Hyaley, & Jesse Manners,
Ana Vicente, Kathleen Longboat, Brandon Pitts,
Brent & Carl Couckuyt, Marc Brown, Mikey Lewis, Dave Whang,
Summer, Olivia, & Savannah Horvat,
Zack Dacosta, Adebe D.A, Bethany G.L, Nirushan, Pamela Yuen, Lee Parpart,
Anthony Stechyson & Michael Strug for looking at some of these
poems in advance.
Michael Catalfamo, Chris Greenhalgh, Aaron France, Chonilal Rishi Maharaj,
    Garry Cormier, & Jamie Jones for
Help & places to stay back in the day.
Steve & Dave Brown, Oliver Weinrib, Georgia Wilder, William Keohane,
Terry Barker, Pat Connors, ROY COHEN,
Bede & Leo McMenamin,
Tamara , Adele & Kids,
David Bateman, & Raymond Helkio, The Lonely Vagabond,
Donnarama, Skyler Longboat,
Dayne Barrett (RIP) Nik Beat (RIP) Sharon & Carl aka "the Bandits" (RIP) &
    Eric Wesley Pentz (RIP)
Nancy Page (RIP) Jordan Manners (Rip)
The Staff at Mosaic Press for helping me make this happen,
The Kitchen party Crew (James, Sheldon, & Chris)
My heroes of the past, Anyone who supported my work,
& again you, for reading this, whoever YOU …are. all the blessings, health &
    triumph, signed

Stedmond Pardy

List of Poetry Readings, & Essential Appearances By Stedmond Pardy

Art Bar poetry series
May 1st, 2023
(with Jade Wallace & Hollay Ghadery)

"Buddies in Bad times" Open mic Feature
April 16th, 2023

National Poetry Month reading/celebration at "the Secret Handshake Gallery"
April 1st, 2023
(with bill bisect, George Elliot Clarke & Honey Novick)

Accent open mic series Vol.56 feature-
October 16th, 2022
(with Jessica Moore & Maria Caltabiano)

Poetry reading at the Imperial Pub
October 5th, 2022
(with David Bateman, & Simon Occulis)

NOWA Events Beaux Arts Brampton-
June 23rd, August 13th 2022
(with Paul Edward Costa, Meena Chopra & others)

Lost Launches -
(with AF Moritz, Andrea Thompson, & others at Clinton's tavern) May 28th 2022

Mosaic Press Book Launch-
(with Pat Connors, & Josie di Scasscio Andrews) May 18th 2022

Minstrels & Bards Spring show-
(with Jennifer Hossein, John Oughton, & others) May 2nd, 2022
Art Bar Poetry series-
(with Carmelo Militano, & Rocco Di Giacomo) March 22th, 2022

SiteLines, OCADU reading & Book Release-
(with Suzanne Stewart) March 20th, 2022

Riverbed Reading series-
(with Unsociably High, & Lillian-Yvonne Bertram) on-line,
Nov.18th, 2020

Brick Books- Brickyard
(with Andrea Thompson, Dave Silverberg, & Leyla Pavao Chisamore)
Supermarket, March 4th, 2020 Toronto, ont.

100,000 POETS FOR CHANGE
(with Pat Connors, Dane Sawn, Marsha Barber, Georgia Wilder, Brenda
Clews, Luciano Iacobelli, Charles C. Smith, & Donna Langevin)
Hirut Restaurant, September 23rd, 2019 Toronto, Ont.

Art Bar Poetry Series
(With Brenda Clews, & Adebe D,A)
Freetimes café, July 9th, 2019 Toronto, Ont.

Ian Ferrier's Words & Music Show
June 30th, 2019 Casa Del Popolo Montreal, Quebec.

The Salon of the Collective creative
(with Lisa de Nikolitis, Ruth Zuchter, Peter Graham, & Nancy
Ceneviva) Annette Street Library Toronto, Ont. April 28th, 2019

Shab-er- Sher Nowruz Celebration
(With Jade Wallace, Padideh Ahrarnejad and Ali Massoud) Tranzac Club, March 26th. 2019
Toronto, Ont.

Secret Handshake Gallery readings
(with Kate DE jong, David Roche, George Zancola) October 28th, 2019 ,
Toronto, ont.

YTGA July open mic at studio.89
July 29th, 2018 Studio 89. Mississauga, Ont.

Love Poetry Festival
(with bill bissett, George Elliot Clarke, Catherine Graham, Michelle Alfano, Domenico Capilongo, Banoo zan, James Daehle, & Norma Linder)
Queen Books, July 28th, 2018, Toronto, ont.

Wild Writers Poetry Series
(With Adebe D.A) May, 1st, 2018 Poetry jazz Café, Toronto, Ont.

One man reading at "the Cineforum"
The Cineforum, September 30th, 2017 Toronto Ont.

Brenda Clews' Poetry & music salon
Fundraiser fort Mcmurray Fire Disaster
Palmerston Library, May 31st, 2016 Toronto, Ont.

Howl 89.5 Ciut Radio
(with Valentino Assenza, & Spencer Butt) May 18th, 2016

Wild Writers poetry series
(With Ellen Jaffe)
Poetry jazz café, july 12th, 2017 Toronto, Ont.

Everett Poetry night
Café zippy, April 20th, 2017 Everett Washington, USA

Dirty Laundry Poetry Series
(with Derkson Dalton, Whitney French,
& Zak Jones) Nov.12th, 2016. Toronto, Ont.

Art Bar Poetry series
(With Roger Greenwall, & Stephanie Yorke)
September 28th, 2016 Freetimes café, Toronto, Ont.

Wild writers Poetry series
(With Myna Wallin)
Poetry jazz café, March 30th, 2016 Toronto, Ont.

Brenda Clews' Poetry Salon
(with Kevin Fortnum & Amoeba Starfish)
Urban Gallery. Feb.28th. 2015 Toronto, Ont.
Art bar Poetry series
(With Max Layton & Benjamin Hackman)
Black swan tavern, March 24th, 2015)

Howl at the Q-space
(With Nik Beat, Norman Allan, & Laura L'Rock)
The Q-space, April 11th, 2013 Toronto, Ont.

One man Reading at "The Cineforum"
March 15th, & 22nd, 2013 Toronto, Ont.

Record vault Reading
(with NIk Beat, Brandon Pitts. Laura DeLeon, Vanessa McGowan, & Laura L'Rock)
The Record vault, October 28th, 2012 Toronto, Ont.

Gadist Poetry Reading
(With Brandon Pitts, & Nik Beat)
Sonic Café, May 27th, 2012 Toronto, Ont.

Howl 89.5 Ciut radio
(with Nik Beat, Saskia Van teetering) April 4th, 2012

Chapbook release & One man reading
Cine cycle July 24th, 2011

Biographical Note

Stedmond Pardy is a self educated, left handed poet of Caribbean Canadian Descent, from Lakeshore Mimico area He has performed his work on stages & radio in Toronto, Alberta, Montreal, & the Seattle/Washington state areas. HIs first full length book of poetry "the Pleasures of this Planet aren't enough" was Published in 2021. He has Released an Audio book to Accompany it, "Beached whales" is his 2nd Book of Poetry Published by Mosaic Press.